AW WITH WORDS

Young Writers' 16th Annual Poetry Competition

It is feeling and force of imagination that make us eloquent.

How can I not dream while writing? The blank page gives a right to dream.

West Sussex
Edited by Annabel Cook

First published in Great Britain in 2007 by:
Young Writers
Remus House
Coltsfoot Drive
Peterborough
PE2 9JX
Telephone: 01733 890066
Website: www.youngwriters.co.uk

All Rights Reserved

© Copyright Contributors 2007

SB ISBN 978-1 84602 836 6

Foreword

This year, the Young Writers' *Away With Words* competition proudly presents a showcase of the best poetic talent selected from thousands of up-and-coming writers nationwide.

Young Writers was established in 1991 to promote the reading and writing of poetry within schools and to the young of today. Our books nurture and inspire confidence in the ability of young writers and provide a snapshot of poems written in schools and at home by budding poets of the future.

The thought, effort, imagination and hard work put into each poem impressed us all and the task of selecting poems was a difficult but nevertheless enjoyable experience.

We hope you are as pleased as we are with the final selection and that you and your family continue to be entertained with *Away With Words West Sussex* for many years to come.

Contents

Burgess Hill School for Girls
Lucy James (16)	1
Philippa Hatendi (17)	2
Lauren Smith (16)	3
Sophia Woodward (15)	4
Isabella Leung (16)	5
Megan Martin (16)	6

Christ's Hospital School
Oliver Clegg (12)	7
Richard Akerele (17)	8
Adam Taylor (12)	9
Cecilia Holden (12)	10
Darcey Haynes (12)	11
Charity Griffiths (11)	12
Jeremiah Nelson (12)	14

Downlands Community School
Abigail McCullough (12)	15
Matthew Vint (12)	16
Brendan Whitmarsh (12)	17
Elizabeth Parkin	18
Jonathan Poncelet (13)	19
Esme Millyard (12)	20
Amy Jackson (12)	21
Chantelle Tovee (12)	22
Emmanuel Latham (12)	23
Victoria Hill (12)	24
Laura Elliston (12)	25
Rebecca Gillespie (12)	26
Luke Miller (12)	27
Emily Wassell (13)	28
Ruby Cooper (12)	29

Ifield Community College
Kyle Tansley (15)	30
Taylor Paddington (14)	31
Nilufer Erdem (14)	32

Katie-Leigh Brown (13)	33
Sophie Cooper (14)	34
Michael Roberts (14)	35
Liam Cooper (14)	36
Mark Hackwell (14)	37
Ryan Ellery (15)	38
Nicole Evans (15)	39
Eloisa Gordon (14)	40
Nuskey Nazeerudeen (14)	41
Joshua Humphreys (14)	42
Mohamed Lazumi (15)	43
Rebecca Cooper (13)	44
Zara Akhtar (13)	45
Sean Reynolds (15)	46
Daniel Austin (15)	47
Paul Lewis (15)	48
Jodie Grinham (13)	49
Zoë Vallance (12)	50
Shannon Robb (13)	51
Jordan French (13)	52
Alexander Patten (12)	53
Jasmin Flint (12)	54
Cona Jackson (12)	56
Joanna O'Connor (12)	57
Shelby Wenham (13)	58
Paige Hobden (14)	59
Nikki Wood (12)	60
Emilee Wright (12)	61
Emma Davey (12)	62
Dean Jones (12)	63
Molly Tucker (12)	64
Katie Hooper (12)	65
Wesley Burd (12)	66
Elliot Higgins (12)	67
Laeek Ahmed (15)	68
Ellesse Tunesi (15)	69
Dylan Bontemps (15)	70
Hayley Cox (11)	71
Charlotte Barnard (11)	72
Nikola Bednarek (11)	73
Cara Bradbury (11)	74
Troy Foster (11)	75

Jake Rose (13)	76
Rebecca Stevenson (12)	77
Gemma Bromley (12)	78
Danielle Mitchell (12)	79
Molly Craven (12)	80
Abigail Cook (12)	81
Stephen Hibbert (12)	82
Matthew McBride (13)	83
Axay Shah (13)	84
Charlie Davis (12)	85
Charlotte Payne (13)	86
Adam Harris (12)	87
Chloe Robinson (12)	88
Zimera Veneziani (12)	89
Livvy Downing (12)	90
Luisa Loureiro (12)	91
James Jarman (13)	92
Tammy Pateman (11)	93
Amber Honisett (13)	94
Hanzlah Abowath (14)	95
Ashlee Smallwood (13)	96
Jessica Pope (13)	97
Charlotte Salmon (13)	98
Melissa Northcott (13)	99
Charlotte Hawes (13)	100
Melissa Pitts (13)	101
Damien Roberts (13)	102
Leanna Marshall (13)	103
Billy Sansom (13)	104
Maxine Smith (11)	105
Jamie Ives (14)	106
Jamie Keay (14)	107
Pritesh Wadher (14)	108
Aaron Finch (13)	109
Hajra Jameel (13)	110
Humail Hussain (13)	111
Kamran Asif (13)	112
Krisjan Boddy (14)	113
Sam Rutter (14)	114
Danielle Johnson (14)	115
Ashlee Saward (11)	116
Adam Lambert (11)	117

John Bye (11)	118
Anna Fraser (11)	119
Chloe Langley (12)	120
Craig Nichols (11)	121
Jack Munday (11)	122
Rebecca Denne (11)	123
Sade Rushton (11)	124
Danny Ellery (11)	125
Chloe Hill (11)	126
George Thorne (12)	127
Thomas Montague-Tompson (11)	128
Joseph Maynard (14)	129
Claudia-Rose Spears (13)	130
Jade Powis (13)	131
Jamie Bridle (13)	132
Adam Dallamore (13)	133
Cheryl Bryant-Owens (14)	134
Daniel Burt (13)	135
Arron Hall (13)	136
Caine Hawkins (13)	137
Ben Logan (13)	138
Krystal Nichols (13)	139
Phillip Hibbert (13)	140
Billy Whinder (13)	141
Chloe Cooke (11)	142
Emily Sidhom (11)	143
Jason Harrold (11)	144
Gary Sawyer (12)	145
Rebecca Wilde (11)	146
William McKnight	147
Cassandra Killner (14)	148
Emma Wiltshire (14)	149
Josh Reeve (13)	150

Millais School

Ana-Maria Braddock (13)	151
Nicky Blyth (13)	152
Natasha Foote (13)	153
Heidi Forster (13)	154
Jessica Langan (13)	155
Siân Ward (13)	156

Hannah Wright (13)	157
Abigail High (13)	158
Charlotte Keegan (13)	159
Lydia Churcher (13)	160
Phoebe Hodges (14)	161
Lucy Ford (13)	162
Emily Colson (13)	163
Georgina Russell (14)	164
Emma Brown (13)	165
Elizabeth Duebel (11)	166
Chloe Hunt (11)	167
Tamsin Romain (12)	168
Charlotte Roadley (11)	169
Chantal Greenfield (11)	170
Anna Betts (11)	171
Francesca Martin (11)	172
Lucy Brogan (11)	173
Leanne Gaffney-Berkeley (11)	174
Nicola Beverton	175
Sarah Benstead (11)	176
Katie Johnston (11)	177
Heather Craig (11)	178
Amy Attwater (12)	179
Sophy Morrow (11)	180
Ashley Kidgell (12)	181
Joanna Canham (12)	182
Amelia Ross (11)	183
Jessica Speller (11)	184
Jasmine Boyce (11)	185
Roya Mandegaran (11)	186
Briony Munslow (12)	187
Kate Wilkinson (11)	188
Molly Eade (12)	189
Matilda Wraith (11)	190
Emily Gardiner (11)	191
Gabrielle Oake (11)	192
Anna Ward (11)	193
Nicola Skelton (11)	194
Hannah Jones (11)	195
Hollie Thomas (12)	196
Emma Griffith (12)	197
Eleanor Simpson (11)	198

Joanna Nayler (12) 199
Zoë Meeks (11) 200
Eve Danbury (11) 201
Emily Lord (11) 202
Kathryn Taylor (11) 203
Rebecca Hollands (12) 204
Lizzie Harman (11) 205

Philpots Manor School
Sarah Porter (17) 206
Emma Wint (17) 207
Megan Simmonds (11) 208

The Poems

Identity

Fading memories of when I was young.
Time passes, new memories created,
Shaping, moulding, sculpting me, the me I wish to forget.
Identity misplaced, out of reach.
Still left in the darkness.
Roots too strong to be ripped out and moved.
No hope of growing again.
Nothing ever changes.
I fought for my freedom -
But still I am a captive of my race, these thoughts
Poisoning my mind that is one brimming black.
Too much love missing, too much love to give.
My beloveds, my beloved, choking with love.
When water refuses to show your reflection
'cause you have no right.
Just a black ink blot on this white piece of paper
needing to be erased,
I am unable to be erased.
Colour drained till we run dry.
Yet that is all I am, a colour, a number, a tool,
Insignificant, uncounted -
Black.

Lucy James (16)
Burgess Hill School for Girls

Twilight

This abyss between light and dark
This fading of the bird's chirp in the trees
Giving unto the silence
And cloaked sounds of night
Stars blink, swathed the inky blackness
This limbo in which I am caught
Between roses and orchids
And the solemn ground beneath them
With its worms and craters . . .
Stories and skulls . . .
From here to home suspended in the air
With my feet on the ground
The feel of water seeping through my hands
The breeze in my lungs
The sunshine on my face
And the cold in my bones
This twilight that holds me in comfort
In fear . . .
This sapphire ink
This space between paper and pen
In which my thoughts scuttle amiss . . .

Philippa Hatendi (17)
Burgess Hill School for Girls

***

Bip. Bip. Bip . . . Bip?
****

Beep. Pin invalid.

*I never was any good
with numbers.
A shame
when you think,
think, think our lives are ruled by them.*

Bip. Bip. Bip . . . Bip?
****

Beep. Pin invalid.

*Were the people who
created this system
elephants?
A wall can't understand
every day people forget,
forget, forget.*

Third time lucky.

Bip. Bip. Bip. Bip.
****

Beep. Card retained. Please contact branch.

****!

Lauren Smith (16)
Burgess Hill School for Girls

Bulimia

I look into the mirror and despise what I see,
The reflection looking back is surely not me.
I walk into the bathroom and turn the radio up loud,
Now no one can hear me and now they have no doubt.

I bend down to the toilet and pull the hair away from my face
Ready to start the torture I feel my heart's increasing pace;
Stabbing my fingers in my throat
I cannot breathe and start to choke.
The burning pain arises and brings all my food back up
But no one can hear me crying as I start to get up.

But later in the mirror I see
A smaller, thinner, more perfect me
Whilst deep within me I am still sad
Why is it that I feel so bad?

The guilt inside of me dwells deep into my heart
The enchantment of destroying myself,
Is tearing my world apart.

Sophia Woodward (15)
Burgess Hill School for Girls

Iden

Romantic indeed.
Walking alone down the road
Packed with earthly mud and earthly snow,
Small flower petals and falling leaves.

I embrace myself into the stirring air
Dreaming of my ambiguity,
And fall back with damn despair
- I reach out my hands for you, Iden,

But you aren't there.

Ironic, isn't it?
Crawling alone in the ground
Crowded with miseries all around,
Filled with dirty mud and expired leaves.

Gently, I let my tears out
And mix them freely with my desire:
Salty, watery liquid melt into sweet fire
Creating a chemical girl

Named 'Ambition'.

Ambi takes my hand.
Her soft skin shines into my bone;
Every bit of it glows,
Echoes and intertwines with a harmonic tone . . .

Fascinating indeed.
Skipping cheerfully down the road,
The two of us hand in hand
In search of identity.

Catch!

I look to seek for your transparent eyes
And lifting the air by my side,
Winging into the wind of
Crashing weather and fearful storms.

Slowly, I reach out my hand for you
With the other hand holding tightly by Ambition.

Isabella Leung (16)
Burgess Hill School for Girls

Branded With Iron

A number so small, insignificant, yet so powerful.

Sizzle, sizzle
Burning, boiling, blistering flesh
Is this world, your one shot, your oyster, your oyster now?
Up,
    Up,
        'Up,
            put these chains round your neck
            round your neck, I say, I, I say I!'
This deep infinite ocean, life, flickers before the eyes.
Dark,
    Dark,
        Dark,
            heavy eyelids *shut*.
Your used-to-be-world gone in a flashhh.
That last, precious, vision of a distant family portrait
        Early 'tis morning,
        Simbawe, Tula
        diggin' in papaya fields;
        'Eave up ye baskets from that dried up ground,
        time to go my loved ones, Mama's got to cook a feast,
        for tomorrow is ya weddin' day
        an early start y'all need.'

Clitter, clatter, clitter, clatter, bang! Bang! Bang!

Time's up, 129, freedom ended at the shore.

Megan Martin (16)
Burgess Hill School for Girls

The Sweeties Are Avenged

A long time ago, in a house made of sweets
a little dog lives, a little dog sleeps
but he didn't know that the sweets were fed up
they came in the night and they gobbled him up.
The sweets were still hungry and they had a plan
they crept in a window and swallowed a man.
The kings of this group, the Twix and the Twirl
invaded a household and swallowed a girl.
They ate the whole town, those troublesome sweets.
All of the buildings and even the streets.
They fought then with the tooth fairy
and threw her down a well
even though she tried to go and break the evil spell.
But in a faraway land now called Namibia
they came into contact with a girl called Lydia.
They charged those little chocolate bars,
the girl, she laughed with mirth,
she then drew out a flame-thrower and fired for all the earth.
Meanwhile Lydia who had had her sweet revenge
had a sudden heart attack: the chocolates were avenged.
The moral of this story is: do not send sweets to hell
or you'll end up like Lydia or the fairy in the well.

Oliver Clegg (12)
Christ's Hospital School

Success

Is success a holy pilgrimage?
Only the holy survive,
The unholy not given a chance to climb up the high hierarchy,
From depth of struggle to the top of the mountain.

Or at least acknowledgement for surviving,
Like a child hungering, awaiting for his mum
When there is nobody there.

Is it for some parts East London vicinity?
That success seems to be a distant island,
A lonely and hard place to reach.
People not willing to climb a ladder
In fear they might fall.
If you do not roll a dice
You cannot get a six.

Is it that the amenities of education are insufficient?
Are they exempt from them?
Or is it that people just see this bare necessity of success
Not attractive or unpopular?

Even though it helps success rain down on their drought.
Like their umbrella against failure.
The question is,
Will they allow this mentality?
Continue to let them believe it is great to be where they are,
Instead of soaring like an eagle despite winds,
Focused on the prey.
This is the only way to succeed.
You just have to believe.

Richard Akerele (17)
Christ's Hospital School

Why?

Why are we here?
It plagues our thoughts,
People come up with answers,
Of all sorts,
Like 'It was God's will',
And 'To rule the Earth'.
But they do not realise
It's just for their mirth,
That people made up these ludicrous things,
It's like saying, 'Oh! I've just sprouted wings!'
Because the true answer,
The real one of course,
Is that aliens did it,
Because they were forced,
By the almighty power of Zaargeltron 8,
A most powerful being who loves to dictate.

Adam Taylor (12)
Christ's Hospital School

Summer Has Come Late This Year

Summer has come late this year,
But it is now slowly fading,
Gently rolling clouds across the bright blue sky,
As if they have a journey to make.

As I can hear the twittering of the birds,
Calling something that we cannot see,
Distant shouting hovering in the air,
With a creeping breeze passing by.

Summer has come late this year,
But now it is slowly fading,
A lonely flower in the pond,
Watches the dragonflies dip their feet in the water.

But above all this calmness I have to say
Is something not as clear,
The day is gently wearing on,
As darkness is very near.

Summer has come late this year,
But now it is slowly fading,
The clock is chiming now,
The day has come to an end,
And summer has come late this year.

Cecilia Holden (12)
Christ's Hospital School

What Am I?

I hear feet. Trailing up the stairs,
Thudding shoes of thunder
As the sound gets closer I pray, 'Please God, not yet another hit.'
I dread the moment that is sure to come,
That tip-tapping sound keeps me waiting in anticipation.
Ouch! - finally the moment has passed and I can see the next villain,
Coming, coming to get me.

There are the shoes that I hate the most,
The shoes of iron,
The shoes covered in mud, that makes my shiny surface so dirty,
Coming straight at me.
I try to move, but evil hands have cruelly nailed me to the floor,
But there is nothing that can save me now.
I can feel my varnish, now peeling,
My worthless wood can take no longer
No one remembers me,
I am forgotten.

Down the stairs I can smell the dinner cooking,
Trying to force myself to think about something else,
        other than my pain
When suddenly
  The constant pulse of hell stops,
  All I hear is my own heartbeat within me

Trembling, I slowly look up,
There he is,
The giant.

What am I?

Darcey Haynes (12)
Christ's Hospital School

Life

If life has meaning what is it?
I mean we are all here together,
But for what?
And why is the hated house wondering about the weather?

If I wasn't wondering about all this,
I'd probably be at home,
Although I don't like the sound,
Of my television, it groans.

If life has meaning what is it?
I mean we are all here together,
But for what?
And why is the hated house wondering about the weather?

I think we are here because God gave us a chance
All of us here on Earth,
Even our angry aunts
And He keeps giving us new birth.

If life has meaning what is it?
I mean we are all here together,
But for what?
And why is the hated house wondering about the weather?

The girls in my dorm are like bubbling birds,
And if they hadn't been bubbling at night,
It wouldn't have given me such a fright.

If life has meaning what is it?
I mean we are all here together,
But for what?
And why is the hated house wondering about the weather?

I wish our fire bell wasn't so strange,
Because it had me outside in the pouring rain.

If life has meaning what is it?
I mean we are all here together,
But for what?
And why is the hated house wondering about the weather?

Do you think that I am right, you think the weather changes?
For I do not know, if I had I would tell you,
And why do you think it snows?

If life has meaning what is it?
I mean we are all here together,
But for what?
And why is the hated house wondering about the weather?
For all I've said is true,
I hope I've helped
And made you think about it too.

Charity Griffiths (11)
Christ's Hospital School

Two Sides

Miaow, miaow he purrs,
He jumps up and scans the area.
Sitting on his posterior,
And cleans his bushy fur.

He starts off poised,
And he leaps up the steep stairs.
Now he's on the landing,
He sprints through the door,
He springs onto the bed.

Miaow, miaow, he purrs,
Digging his claws into their skin.
Her head elevates from under the duvet,
He recoils, because she looks scraggy,
Oh well! He still licks her on the face.

He thinks, *look there's an open window.*
Next minute he is put off it,
Off the ledge then off the walls, now he's gone!

He's a little six dinner Sid,
He dines at Margaret's, next minute Ellie's,
Then Mrs Robinson's, although it's getting dark,
He's still out for more.
'Felix' at Lucy's, then some fish from the old lad,
Then back to his owner's house,
For a bit more of that treat.

Then he's off out again, sitting on the pavement,
Then the cars drive past,
There were his eyes glaring in the dark,
Then, as the light touches his eyes, he stretches then runs away.

Off up the alley he goes, in the alley, then he sees a bin,
There's a cat opposite him, eyeing the bin up and down as well,
He makes the first move,
Violently moving they knock a metal dustbin,
The cats now are found, the guy separates,
And takes him back to his owner whose house is two doors away,
But the other cat, he keeps.

Jeremiah Nelson (12)
Christ's Hospital School

Time Of Loneliness

Time of loneliness, harsh and hard.
Death of summer leaves a desolate world.
Silent and empty, muffled by frost.
Frost like thorns, a blanket of quiet
Suffocating the Earth in its icy hands.

Skies are grey, bleak and bare.
Mist clings to skeletal trees like a shroud,
Their bones are stripped and bare.
Twigs jut out like ghostly fingers,
Piercing the air with their dark tendrils.

Leaves rustle ominously underfoot.
Dead and decomposing, they lie in a heap
Piles of limp bodies that have fallen.
The living are dying, hanging from branches,
Oozing scarlet like blood.

The air warns the world with a frozen bite,
Sending the globe into hibernation.
Starting the death of nature.
Autumn. The end of the beginning.
The beginning of the end.

Abigail McCullough (12)
Downlands Community School

Autumn

Elegant summer colours,
Bold muscular trees,
Decorated nature,
Slowly leaves.

The vulnerable branches break,
The leaves die away,
Conkers are ready to take,
Autumn is coming your way.

Beautiful strands of lush green grass,
Ripe fruit trees grow at last,
Amazing leaves made of brass,
The miraculous sun is not yet the past.

But as the sunbeams fade,
Rotten apples die away,
New leaves are eventually made,
Winter is coming your way.

Matthew Vint (12)
Downlands Community School

Autumn

Summer's tyranny starts to fade,
As Autumn comes to power.
The parched trees freed of their burden,
And their thirst quenched with rain.

The leaves flutter slowly down,
Littering the ground, a rustling carpet.
A light in the morning mist,
Protection for the vulnerable grass.

The slugs and snails begin to wake,
Safe from wicked birds and badgers.
They make their way along the sunlit leaves,
And bathe in the dim light of the clouded sun.

Brendan Whitmarsh (12)
Downlands Community School

Winter's Conquest

Silver lady.
Flees.
Across a darkening sky.
Fleeing the snow
And the jaws of frost.
She can feel the death
It brings.

One left.
One.
Holding on with weakening
Fingers. Winter
Mocks. And Death
Surrounds the poor oak tree.
Falling. Falling.

The night
Weeps.
The last leaf fallen.
Frozen tears hung
From the last branch
Mist rises
It is Winter's domain . . .

Elizabeth Parkin
Downlands Community School

Autumn

Autumn.
Brown leaves falling,
A funeral of summer but at the same time a birthday for new plants.
Conkers dropping, their surface gleaming,
Millions of acorns cover the grass in a crunchy carpet.
Trees begin to brown,
Animals store food for the winter.
The nights get darker; mist clouds the air every morning.
Soon winter will arrive,
Bringing cold winds, snow, ice . . .
Christmas.

Jonathan Poncelet (13)
Downlands Community School

Autumn Is Death Of The Summer

Autumn is death of the summer,
The beginning of the end,
Domesday,
But underneath all that,
The beauty of autumn shines through,
Which softens the blow,
Spiderwebs with dewdrops resting on the silk,
Ruby-red leaves blowing gently in the harsh wind,
Acorns dangling off the trees wearing little berets,
Conkers with a spiky armour,
But inside is smooth and shiny,
A rich chocolate-brown,
Reflecting the light,

The death of the summer,
But the beginning of something new,

Leaves vary in colour, shape and size,
Plums and purples, aubergines and oranges,
All vivid and colourful,
Fruits and flowers, ripe and ready to eat,

Beautiful animals, insects and birds come out in autumn,
Preparing for hibernation,
Fluorescent caterpillars with spiky bodies,

Autumn is death of the summer,
The beginning of the end,
Doomsday,

But it doesn't have to be.

Esme Millyard (12)
Downlands Community School

Bird's-Eye View

I swoop,
Swoop across the leaves.
I hear a creaking below.
I glance down and see trees shudder.
A single creature struggles on alone.
I weep,
Weep for all that is lost as autumn arrives.
Spider webs no longer inhabited.
Abandoned for the winter.
As they try to save their necks.
I choke,
Choke back my tears.
I try to drive my sadness away.
Cold frosts claim lives
My heart feels for those innocent creatures
So unaware of what is soon to come.
I wish,
Wish I could warn them.
But I must live on.
To tell tales of this tragedy
And maybe fly again
I call,
Call the birds in front,
I am alone
I must carry this grief alone.
But I know,
Know my task is to tell.
To watch and to inform.
I let out a last mournful cry
And I am gone.

Amy Jackson (12)
Downlands Community School

Finding Acorns

A strong wind whirls the leaves in a hurricane,
As they tumble from the mighty trees,
Acorns dropping on the ground,
Propelling leaves, piling over them, protecting from prying predators,
Birds swooping down and pecking at worms,
But I have another meal on my mind,
I scurry down the great oak from where I watched,
Then leaped down onto the crumbling leaves,
I dug around, and underneath,
My bushy tail standing when I find success,
My sharp teeth gnaw deep into its hard shell,
It was satisfying,
I carry on racing around collecting acorns,
I hide them from other hungry creatures of the forest,
Then racing off to watch out again,
Before winter attacks.

Chantelle Tovee (12)
Downlands Community School

The Little Acorn Soldier

Born, born in summer,
Born to battle out the winter,
But sent to fight in autumn.
With his hard rough helmet on
He marches from,
From the tree, his place of birth
To rule, to continue his race
In another wooded place,
Not knowing the journey in hand.
He drops, rolls, takes cover on the ground,
Marching his strong green body out to fight for life,
Then, then *bang!* Killed, buried, dead.
The conqueror, the conker that took his life holds him down.
He shrivels under its weight,
Slowly blackness overcomes his brittle body.

'Here lies Private Oak,
The dead leader of Hassocks' grandest oak'.

Emmanuel Latham (12)
Downlands Community School

Autumn

Stripped trees as bare as flesh,
Standing in blankets of flaming reds,
Surrounded by crispy winds,
Showering,
Smothering them.

Dew on the grass, just starting to settle,
As the dying sun gives one last shine of light and heat
To last the day.

The flaky leaves sway from side to side,
As they tumble delicately to the ground,
Showing the summer's end.

The glossy light,
Shimmering off the satin silk thread,
While the maker is collecting food.
These will search and kill for warmth
As the heat is no longer produced.

I think of it as, a funeral, as such,
Only life is not lost as it shall come again.

Nothing is lost,
Nothing has gone,
For all shall return,
A new life has been born as another has ended
Creating a new world.

Victoria Hill (12)
Downlands Community School

Autumn

Hollow mists and whispering through the oaks:
The death of summer.
But a reminder that Nature is still alive.

Ghostly, silvery webs of spiders
Glittering like diamonds in the morning dew.
Soft spiky horse chestnut shells.
Delicate shapes of fallen leaves:
Crinkled, curling, dancing, swirling
Crimson and bronze and gold and red,
Dustily resting on the cold earth.
Cool, smooth acorns nestling,
Ripening in their gentle cups.
Shimmering wishes of summer's ghosts,
And softly the rain kisses the milky sky.

At night the sky is majestic
And in its velvet, pinpricks shine.
In the pink of dawn, the night unfolds,
And soft as cotton, pussy willow in the lane,
With scarlet berries on the greying twigs.
A cold, hard bite of icy frostiness circles through the air,
And chestnuts ripe scatter the ground.

Shimmery mist veils the hills,
Concealing and mysterious.
White grass, creamy with sharp frost,
And grey, sweet, icy skies frame an enchanting picture.

Half-ripe crab apples adorn this silvery world,
Pink yet sour inside,
Waiting to be picked,
In the death of summer.

But Nature will always survive.

Laura Elliston (12)
Downlands Community School

Red Light Of Fall

Season of mists and abundance,
mellow red lights of fall warm the earth
burning the world's fiery hearth.

To pull the crops from the brown turned land
giving the soil's children to the air.

The world's eyes burn with crimson fire,
flaming with the ripples of scarlet tears,
wept from the branches of maple trees.

The rich smells of fallen mackintosh,
filled with ripened fruitfulness to the core.

Berries swell and the dust from harvested grain.
Pumpkins swell and blood spills from the forest fruits.

Sparkling jewels litter the tired land.
For the year is old
and the geese grow bold.
Their song vibrates through the sun.

Rebecca Gillespie (12)
Downlands Community School

Autumn Days

As we pull on our lovely warm coats
The tall trees lose their golden ones
Dancing through the air
To create a blanket
For the shimmering, dew covered grass

The magnificent oaks
Lose their smooth brown acorns
They mourn and they choke
Their loved ones all depart

But the small animals
Are happy for the loss
Because they can gather their food
For the cold is beginning to start

The reds, greens and pinks
Turn darker and richer
Gold, brown and yellow they turn
While people sit at home and wonder
'Where has the summer gone now?'

The winds that are now much stronger
Blow leaves across the globe
And their rich and beautiful colours
Are there for all to enjoy

Autumn is a wonderful thing
That brings the start to many new things
But people always forget
The loss it also brings.

Luke Miller (12)
Downlands Community School

Autumn

Autumn, the season of thoughtfulness,
The slow, dying season.

Mellow fruits and soft berries
Drop and return to the earth
Crisp curling leaves fall
Gently, soundlessly floating
In the cool fresh breezes.

Misty, mysterious dawn
Revealing the fires of colour
As the trees weep
For their dear departed.

The bees rejoice in shimmering meadows
The crickets tire in dappled shadows
Squirrels scamper, collecting
Chestnuts, conkers, acorns
Ripe in downy white cups and shells.

The essence of autumn
The dying of summer.

Emily Wassell (13)
Downlands Community School

The Market

A light patter of feet against the stone,
The traders scurry to and fro,
As note by note, tone by tone,
The market begins its long crescendo,
A kaleidoscope of colour is emerging,
Busy bees are swarming around stalls,
By now the market place is surging,
And the climax of the bazaar bawls.
A rushed patter of feet against the stone,
Buyers scurry to and fro
As note by note, tone by tone,
The market begins its diminuendo.
The buyers scrape the last of the wares,
The rainbow fades into the mist,
All traders retire to their chairs,
The market, no longer sun-kissed.
A light patter of feet against the stone,
Traders scurry to and fro,
As note by note, tone by tone,
The market ends its diminuendo.

Ruby Cooper (12)
Downlands Community School

Football

Onto the football pitch, full of hope.
Thinking of the chance you have to win.
The whistle blows to start the game,
The pace gets faster as it starts to rain.

Tackles go in but some are harsh,
Sliding through the puddles and the grass.
A goal goes in and our hopes all die,
As our goalkeeper, Lewis, begins to cry.

The goals pour in as our heads drop
Half-time goes as we all stop,
The manager thinks we're beginning to flop,
He thinks when we're near we should have a pop.

The whistle goes to start again,
As we got our heads in the game.
In one huge great stride,
We regained our pride.

8-1 was the end score,
As we walked out the door,
We left with our heads held high,
It's a good job we decided to try.

Kyle Tansley (15)
Ifield Community College

As The Rubber Burned And The Sirens Wailed

As the rubber burned and the sirens wailed,
The copper conning convicts once again had failed,
The radio called in backup for two,
As the getaway car flipped with its four man crew.

The car 25 screeched to a halt,
And out they stepped on an on foot assault,
Out crept criminals, guns at the ready,
Taking cover their guns all steady.

Bullets flying overhead underneath,
Until the bullet hit the thief,
He fell to the floor clutching his neck,
Out stepped SWAT, all heads on deck.

The convicts ducked, trying to heal,
Positions taken, prepared to kill,
Oil leaked and bullets fired
Sparks turned into flames and the convicts died,

As the rubber burned and the sirens wailed.

Taylor Paddington (14)
Ifield Community College

Relationships

What's the point?
Who wants to know?
When your heart is broken,
And you're at your lowest low.

You give up so much,
When for them it's just lust,
Your time, personal secrets and trust,
Then it all goes down that bitter lane,
With your falling tears like rain,
What you both did together
And how sweet it became.

You were so comfortable around them,
Felt safe even when vulnerable,
Pain never crossed your mind,
Being alone wasn't real,
But now that you're alone,
How does it feel?

Hurt? Weak? Used? Lost?
Exactly how much does your dignity cost?
It better be worth as much as you felt,
For you lost it through the love that you dealt.

Nilufer Erdem (14)
Ifield Community College

My World In World War I

We all watch where we're going so we don't get seen,
As we all cough up blood we stagger along,
As I try to get to safety and some rest,
All I can hear in the background is them screaming,
But the noise slowly fades,
The men are so exhausted and with no hope in their eyes,
They can hardly walk,
And their clothes look like they have been dragged
                              through a bush backwards,
But they just keep walking,
Not knowing there are gas shells falling behind us,
'Quick men, put your gas mask on,
Poisonous gas heading our way!'
As I fumble with my gas mask,
The green cloud coming towards us,
I get the gas mask on just in time,
But one man is unlucky and starts choking,
I can't do anything, it's hopeless, he's dying,
The gas is like greenish-coloured stained golden syrup,
I can only see tunnel vision,
So I can't see my friends properly and don't know if they're OK,
The man runs towards me,
I can't do anything,
I try to put his gas mask on for him,
But it doesn't make any difference,
He is being carried on a wagon,
He's choking,
His face looks like he's just seen a ghost but worse,
How would you feel if you had to do this?
He looks like he's being electrocuted, he jumps and gags,
And all you lot say 'it's glorious to die for your country',
And all that stuff I got told was a shamble,
I saw someone dying a horrible death today,
He did not die a glorious death at all!

Katie-Leigh Brown (13)
Ifield Community College

One Devotion

When I was down, you lifted me up,
When I never had the chance, you never gave up.
You are always there for me.
Gazing upon me, lovingly.

We shared the pain,
The sorrow,
The anxiety.
Day by day and tomorrow.

You are my one hope,
One love,
One faith,
One destiny,
One heart.

The cold feeling I get when you're not there,
How it changes so rapidly when you are near.
I look into your deep dark eyes,
I feel safe, protected.
I feel that tingly feeling you get when you're in love.

Ti amo, (Italian)
J'adore tu, (French)
Te quiero, (Spanish)
Is what I feel about you.

You are my destiny for all eternity.
The shining star in my midnight sky.
The light in my Broadway.

The way I feel about you is indescribable,
The way you look at me,
The way you treat me,
The way you feel about me,
The way you care about me,
The way you adore and treasure me.

My passion towards you burns like fire.
My one and only desire.

Sophie Cooper (14)
Ifield Community College

Hopes And Dreams

I lay silently on my bed,
Many thoughts in my head.
What will I do with my life?
How will I meet my demise?

Rock star, actor, what will I be?
Do I even know that fame is for me?
I could be stuck in a dead-end job,
Or become a couch potato slob.

Let's get back to positive things,
Mercedes Benz and diamond rings.
Showcase wives and classy clothes,
Hummers and jeeps to rule the road.

As I think of my hopes and dreams,
I wonder what my life means.
Is there a future for you and me?
I'll guess we'll both have to wait and see.

Michael Roberts (14)
Ifield Community College

Last Friday

The longest day of the week,
Will I turn old and weak?
Yesterday ended but will today,
When Joanie has a debt to pay?

She reaches the front door,
His dead body spread across the floor,
Will she meet her own demise?
Can't hold her emotions and cries.

She runs and runs but cannot escape,
When his murderer reaches her front gate,
She hides in her bed and tries to ignore,
The banging on her bedroom door.

She plucks up courage and takes a peek,
Only the thing in front of her is a freak!
When midnight has struck and her cries are gone,
And all she wanted was to hear his song . . .

Liam Cooper (14)
Ifield Community College

Christmas Time

Christmas time, Christmas time,
Is a time to jump and joy,
Some countries go out on their sleighs,
While other countries don't go out on cold days,
Friends and family give presents to one another,
While the weather is not a bother,
People hang up their Christmas decorations,
While in Africa there are food deliverations,
Christmas time is the time to enjoy,
So make the most and like the days.

Mark Hackwell (14)
Ifield Community College

The Big Bully

The big bully lives at school
The big bully looks cruel
The big bully looks confused
The big bully could blow a fuse.

The big bully looks tough
But I bet he is all bluff
I wouldn't say that to his face
Then he will look at me as a disgrace.

Ryan Ellery (15)
Ifield Community College

Cause Of Death: Broken Heart

She screamed out in pain
She screamed out his name.
Clutching her side like a claw of an eagle
To stop the flow, but nothing would.
Tears fell as she wept
But her hope she still kept,
Who knew one bullet could cause so much ache
But the fast growing wound was not her final call.
Her insides were out, on the side of the street
From her body fast, she was losing heat,
But the gaping, pulsing hole was not the true pain
The fact that *he* had done it crushed her heart.
She lay in a lake of her own bloody past
Her movement was slowing, faster than fast,
Confusion fell upon those looking ahead
How did this girl come to have
A deadly gunshot to her side?
Yet a broken heart is how she died.

Nicole Evans (15)
Ifield Community College

Dwelling On A Fantasy

When I'm dwelling on a fantasy,
Nothing else seems like reality.
My mind gives it credibility,
Blocking out all deficiencies,
Focusing intently on the amenity.
I deny myself of all insecurities
And bathe in the purity,
Chasing the innocence with cupidity.
In life, this peace is an anomaly.
So I cling to it possessively,
Letting myself lapse into coveted serenity.
In a dream, I can hide from asperity,
Cloaking myself from hostility
And disappear from this world of tedious tendencies.
I often lose myself in the lure of its beauty,
When I'm dwelling on a fantasy.

Eloisa Gordon (14)
Ifield Community College

One Day

Start of the twenty-second century,
Six decades after the blue whales' extinction,
Five after the elephants,
Four after the fossil fuels.

The land around me has the heat to fry us,
The atmosphere near me has the power to crush us.
Still we survive,
Thanks to technology.

Trees, we see in museums,
Tablets, we have on our lunch tables,
Hover pods, we race within grand stadiums,
Hearts, we sold for our survival.

But one day I'll see animals again,
One day I'll breathe unpaid oxygen again,
One day I'll see rivers again,
One day I'll go to Earth

From this lonely artificial planet.

Nuskey Nazeerudeen (14)
Ifield Community College

Why?

Why in the world is there war?
If you ask me, it is quite a bore.
Two or more sides fighting endlessly.
If you ask me, it is done pointlessly.

Pollution is caused by men like me.
Driving taxis, buses and a Lamborghini.
Energy consumption is too rapidly done
But if it carries on, there will be no fun,
Just think of it that way.

Conservation of the natural world
Is our responsibility in the world.
In 20 years' time we could find
The tiger, elephant and whale alike
Could be found all dead as corpses.

Violence in homes around the globe
Continue to happen even though
We don't want it to
So why not stop it, don't let it go?

Why are all these things present on Earth?
In New York, London and Australia's Perth.
We can stop them, so why not?
I would like someone to answer my questions . . .
Why, why, why on Earth?

Joshua Humphreys (14)
Ifield Community College

I Love To Fly

I love to fly
I could be a bird
But if I was a bird
They would catch me
And put me in a cage

I fly free in the clouds
As high as the stars
The sky is wide
I love to fly

I fly at night
The sky is black
Covered in stars
I feel scared
But I still love to fly.

Mohamed Lazumi (15)
Ifield Community College

Mum

My mum is like an angel
My mum is like a star
And when I am down she is there beside me.
She's like a flowing river in my heart
That's why she is so special to me,
That's why she's so special to me.

Rebecca Cooper (13)
Ifield Community College

Goodbye Friend

You made me laugh,
You dried my tears,
Because of you
I have no fear,
Together we live,
Together we grow,
Teaching each other
What we must know.
You came into my life,
What a blessing that was,
I love you friend
You are the best.
Release my hand
And say goodbye,
Please my friend
Don't you cry.
I promise you this
It's not the end,
Like I said
You are my friend.

Zara Akhtar (13)
Ifield Community College

A Bird

I see a bird in full flight,
It flew towards the light,
Then it disappeared out of sight.

Its beak hooked,
But sharper than it looked,
To scare and spook,
Its prey as loot.

A bird praying for a mouse,
But all it could find is a house,
Or could it be looking for its spouse.

Sean Reynolds (15)
Ifield Community College

Phoenix

The phoenix is a mythical bird,
Surrounded by flames and fire,
When it sings it can be heard.

It flies so beautifully in the air,
Its rainbow wings fill the sky,
Above us all without a care.

It kills itself in a ball of fire,
But it's reborn as a chick,
To live again to soar the sky.

Daniel Austin (15)
Ifield Community College

Thinking Thoughts

If you're thinking of nothing,
You're not thinking at all.
If you can't think of anything,
Try to think of something.
If you're thinking of something,
What is it you're thinking of?
If you can't think of nothing,
You are thinking of everything.
Thoughts, thoughts,
Always running through my mind.
I can't think of nothing, not thought before,
As I've thought my last thought.
Now my thought is gone.
I'm thinking of another thought.
This one already thought,
By another thinker.
I think that sounds wrong,
But I think it sounds right.
I thought, I thunk a thought,
But I can't think a thought as of before,
As a thunk thought goes away,
To make room for other thoughts to be thunk.

Paul Lewis (15)
Ifield Community College

My Dream

I dream that I have
a great big pet whale,
with a money squirting blow hole
and a solid gold tail.

I'd be rich in money,
animals and pets,
he wouldn't need clothes,
cleaning out or the vets.

I could swim with my whale,
all over the Seven Seas,
and all over the world,
from England to Swansea.

Jodie Grinham (13)
Ifield Community College

Polar Bears

Polar bears are fluffy and white,
They play all day and sleep at night.
After they've slept and it's now the day,
They have to go out and hunt their prey.
Before they go out in the snow and play,
They feed their cubs and eat their prey.

Zoë Vallance (12)
Ifield Community College

Love

Love is a feeling between you and another
It may be your friend, it may be your lover
Love can be happiness
Love can be fun
But it can also be painful when love comes undone.
All these feelings you build up inside
All come out at the blink of an eye.
You think it's your life
You think it's your world
Just never forget there are other people as well.

Shannon Robb (13)
Ifield Community College

Harvest Festival

When you see the children on the telly,
each one has a hungry belly.
Then you think of all the food you have
a tin of beans, a packet of crisps
even a 20p could help.

Anything is good enough just for them
to go to bed nice and full.

There they can look forward to the day ahead
with a nice breakfast.
So go on, be a part of it,
the harvest festival.

Jordan French (13)
Ifield Community College

Toto

As cute as a bunny,
As vicious as a lion.
As black as night,
As soft as silk.
As naughty as a monkey,
As funny as a clown.
As chatty as a parrot,
As bouncy as a ball.
He really is so funny,
That's my cat.

Alexander Patten (12)
Ifield Community College

My Lair

My story is unwritten
My story is untold
But soon you will see
My story unfold.

A haunted house
Comes into your sight
You look at a window
There beams out a light.

A shadow moves
You look away
Too scared to see
If you're its prey.

But then you look
The light has gone
Did you imagine it?
Were you wrong?

Then you thought
I have to find out
You pushed the gate
There was no one about.

You knocked on the door
'Is anyone there?'
Not noticing that
You have entered my lair.

The damp and wet ceiling
And creaky wood floors
Webs in the corners
Of decaying wood doors.

Rustic old keys
Knocking of knees.
Locks which are broken
Secrets unspoken.

Secrets will be
Secrets no more,
For you know them now
But not anymore . . . !

Jasmin Flint (12)
Ifield Community College

World War II

Noses are red,
My feet are blue,
There's lice in my pants,
And the rats ate the stew,
But I'm alive.

Thank God.

The trenches are quiet,
The guns asleep,
The Germans at bay,
And I'm alive.

Thank God.

The artillery fires,
The whistle blows,
We rise up from our pit,
And off we go,
We charge German lines,
Guns blazing all the time,
Then a beautiful sight,
The Huns turn and ran,
And we have won,
And I'm still alive.

Thank God.

Cona Jackson (12)
Ifield Community College

Nightmares!

Wind whistling,
Lights flashing,
Spiders crawling,
Body shivering!

Floorboards creaking,
Trees rustling,
Loud shrieking,
Teeth shaking!

Curtains flapping,
Moon beaming,
Door squeaking,
I gasp!

Joanna O'Connor (12)
Ifield Community College

Destiny

Everything happens for a reason,
but if you fall at something that could break your dream,
should you try again?

Aiming for something can shove you back,
pushing yourself to the max every day
for something you may never reach,
is it worth it?

Fate is a funny thing,
churning and changing things forever.

Can you push past it?
How far will you go to reach your destiny?

Shelby Wenham (13)
Ifield Community College

The Missing Homework

One day when I went to school
my teacher asked me why I had not done my homework.
So I said, 'Sorry Sir, my homework is dead.
My dog chewed it up while I was in bed.
I looked for it everywhere in the morning
but my dog had it hanging out of his mouth
while he was snoring.
I tried to pull it out but it was no good
it was stuck down his throat
so I got my mum to write you a note.
So that is why my homework is not done,
and here is that note from my mum.'

Paige Hobden (14)
Ifield Community College

Emotions

Love beyond love
Hate above hate
They are both emotions
That make us wait

When it is winter
And we are cold
We think of love
And we behold
A warmth like no other
That stays in the heart.

But when we are bored
We think of hate
Something rears in our chest
That makes us bait
Until we look at our friendship
That's broken in two.

We find ourselves sad
(An emotion too)
But happiness counters it
And we find ourselves thinking
Why look at the bad things
When happiness is blinking.

Nikki Wood (12)
Ifield Community College

Whoosh!

Winds whirling
Waves crashing
Windows smashing
Whoosh!

Cars upturned
People flying
Trees blowing
Whoosh!

Animals hiding
Children crying
Insects dying
Whoosh!

A splash of light
A feeling of fright
Wrecked up kites
Whoosh!
The storm is over.

Emilee Wright (12)
Ifield Community College

Exit Out Of Earth

I sat down on the floor
Wondering what went wrong
Wondering what had happened
When the beat of my heart was gone.
It all started in the taxi
From work to bring me home.
No one else but the driver
I am glad I was alone.
For when the girl ran in front of the car
I thought, *oh no, dear Lord!*
But we swerved into a building
When the tyres moved of their own accord.
I waited in the wreckage
Until sirens were heard, an ambulance was near
But the car exploded before and I ended up right here.

Emma Davey (12)
Ifield Community College

Come On England!

I was driving down the road
In my shiny red car
I caught a glimpse of the football
England hit the bar!
I had to get home fast
I had to watch the game
20 minutes had already passed
And I was going insane
As soon as I got in
I turned the TV on
I'm just in time to see the goal
Peter Crouch is on a roll.

Dean Jones (12)
Ifield Community College

The Cat Lady

She sits in her chair,
With her long silver hair,
Little does she know,
That we all stop and stare.

At the bus stop I sat
And I noticed on her hat
Sat a little ginger cat.

There isn't just one colour
But black, white and grey,
They just come out in summer
And only for one day.

The old lady is still there today
And the cats are there to stay,
There is no more that I can say
Just farewell and good day.

Molly Tucker (12)
Ifield Community College

Insects

Bees whizz
Slugs fizz
Ants hurry
Bugs scurry
Crickets hop
Cockroaches pop
Wasps sting
Butterfly's wing
Spiders build
Ticks revealed
Moths rest
Ladybirds test
Mayflies utter
Dragonflies flutter
Woodworms squiggle
Ordinary worms wiggle.
At the end of the winter
Most will be dead
At the beginning of the spring
Most of them will get out of bed.

Katie Hooper (12)
Ifield Community College

Birds

When ice covers the distant land,
These creatures face it first hand.
Scavenging in rain and sun,
Accepting weather as it comes.

Making firm nests in trees,
Flying, gliding overseas.
Making a nest in a house,
Seeking carefully for a minute mouse.

Eagles looking elegant,
Pecking fleas off an elephant.
Baby woodpeckers looking well fed,
Pecking twigs into place to make a bed.

Covets looking cautiously,
Scanning the waters carefully.
Mating,
Skating.

With their delicate wings,
How well the jolly bird loves to sing.
Wind drifting under wing,
Flying in a circular ring.

Eating insects,
Injuries to inflict.
Dodging,
Fledging.

Migrating in the crisp orange fall,
Returning gleefully with their own small.

Wesley Burd (12)
Ifield Community College

Tiger

Tigers come out at day
When there's lots of animals at play.
They've slept for eighteen hours
And now need food for powers.

They hunt all alone
As they want to be king of the throne.
They use their stripes to hide
And their time they abide.

They see their prey
And they're on their way.
They run, they jump, they strike,
The feast has just begun.

Elliot Higgins (12)
Ifield Community College

My First Priority

My family is my first priority, they mean the world to me.
My family are the ones who will be there for me
in my good and bad times,
they will try to be there while they can.
If they're not here there is no point for me to be here.
If my family leave me in life my heart will be broken in pieces
and it will be hard to be put back together.
The only people I have caring for me are my family.

Laeek Ahmed (15)
Ifield Community College

My Boyfriend

I look at my boyfriend
then I look at me,
without my honey where will I be?
My friends, my boys, my shadow, my world
where will I be without my boy?
Tears, giggles, smiles and laughs,
late night calls and cute photographs.
I'll be there for you till the day of my death
together, forever until my very last breath.

Ellesse Tunesi (15)
Ifield Community College

A Girl Like You

How did I get a girl like you?
A girl that's smart, pretty and true.
A girl that I can hold.
A girl that is 'just right'.

A girl that can make me happy.
A girl that is nice and wise.
A girl that I would never forget.
A girl that will stay in my heart.

A girl that I can love forever and always.
A girl that doesn't need to give anything.
A girl that is really calm.
A girl that can understand me.
A girl that I don't need to give any money.

Dylan Bontemps (15)
Ifield Community College

Shoes

S ome people like them, some hate them.
H eels are my favourites.
O pen-toed shoes also look good.
E ither for boys or girls.
S ummer shoes are nice to wear.

Hayley Cox (11)
Ifield Community College

Boys Will Be Boys

Boys will be boys because they always make a noise.
Sometimes they are chubby and thick.
They try to kiss anyone they meet.

Boys will be boys because they always make a noise.
Always shouting, always wrestling, always killing.

Boys will be boys because they always make a noise.
Always showing off, always impressing girls but they are caring.
And that is why boys are boys.

Charlotte Barnard (11)
Ifield Community College

The Snake

I'm a snake, not a worm,
I look like one, but I'm not,
People think that I am nasty,
But that's really not true.

I'm a snake, not a worm,
I look like one, but I'm not,
I'm a friendly little snake,
I'm afraid of big bears.

I'm a snake, not a worm,
I look like one, but I'm not,
I want to play with little children,
But people think that I will bite them.

Nikola Bednarek (11)
Ifield Community College

The Dolphin

The dolphin swims gracefully through the ocean
as the waves tumble over.

The dolphin splashes as she dives through the frozen water
underneath her fins sleek along quietly.

She gains her speed to do somersaults
under and over the tumbling waves.

Her tail is long and blue,
dark and light reflects in the shimmering water.

Cara Bradbury (11)
Ifield Community College

Dragons

My teeth are sharp
My claws are as strong as steel cages
My tail is a sharp sword
My skin's a flamey red, as bright as a ruby
My eyes are a burnt black, like dark orbs
My back is a barbed fence
My feet are giant duck feet
I am my own fiery fury!

Troy Foster (11)
Ifield Community College

The School Play

Every day, every day
We practice for the school play.

The play's name is IQ-Zero
And tells the story of one hero.

His name is No-Brains
And he used to be a plumber working on drains.

He is played by Brian Hego
Who has the same IQ as his alter ego.

Then there's Dr Insane
Who has an extremely large brain.

He is played by Michael Stud
Who hates being the bad guy and calls it crud.

Then there's me, little old me
Who is insignificant as can be.

For you see
All I play is a small baby.

This is the story in my eyes
It is so sad I start to cry.

Because I am only aged zero
And will never be a hero.

Jake Rose (13)
Ifield Community College

My Bearded Dragon

I have a bearded dragon called Ziggy
he's such a little sweetie.
He is very small but rapidly growing,
eating a balanced diet containing chirping insects
and lots of leafy greens.
His scales are like a sunset, rich in red.
When the lights go out he tucks up for bed.

Rebecca Stevenson (12)
Ifield Community College

Up So High

The stars are shining in the sky,
Up, up, up so high.
Like a rocket shooting by,
I wave goodbye as they fly.
Up they go into space
With their suitcase.
They will be back once again,
But when?

Gemma Bromley (12)
Ifield Community College

Crazy

Have you ever stopped to think
If all the world was baby pink
And all the clouds
Could speak out loud
And all the cats and dogs
Would always hop and jog
All the cows and pigs
Were as small as a twig
And all the humans had fleas
Wow what a crazy world that would be.

I'm going crazy!

I'm going mad
Today I saw a fish get really sad
Then I saw 2 pigs dancing
Then came along 4 cows prancing
I swear I saw a mole rat fly
Then a floating banana in the sky
Then I saw a field mouse being lazy
My word, I must be going crazy.

Danielle Mitchell (12)
Ifield Community College

The Nightmare Creature

The creature that is very rotten
We all hope can be forgotten,
But he stays there in your mind
Like a picture left behind,
When thought of him won't be gone
Until his night job is done,
This job he has is full of tears
Which he has made and people fear,
His job is cruel and very unfair.
His job is being your worst nightmare.

Molly Craven (12)
Ifield Community College

Clear Blue Surfer

Blue and clear, sometimes icy cold,
The way the waves twist and fold.
The white foam sprays away,
The sand under water it lays.

The fish are startled, and away they swim,
Suddenly I see a dark grey fin.
I look around and see it disappear,
It evaporates, that is my fear,
I skim the waves like a pebble on a lake,
The waves are big that the sea makes.

Under a curl of a wave,
Like my private watery cave.
I touch the water, with my hand,
All of a sudden I'm back on the watery sand.

I grab my board and run back out,
I know another wave like that will be back,
Without a doubt.

Abigail Cook (12)
Ifield Community College

The Metallic Blue . . .

A car that catches wind like paper through the air . . .
A car that is built for speed . . .
A car that speeds like a 1st class jet plane . . .
It's the Mazda RX8.

The car that avoids corners . . .
The car that has devastating power . . .
The car that doesn't need nitrous . . .
It's the Mazda RX8.

It's always the car that claims victory . . .
It's always the car that can't get dents . . .
It's always the car that gets popularity . . .
But it might not be the Mazda RX8.

Stephen Hibbert (12)
Ifield Community College

Me And My Dog

I have a dog you know . . .
his name is Lucky you know
he's quite the average dog I think
not many people know him
he's like my secret.

I feed him and play with him
it's very fun watching him
he loves it when I stroke him
I like to feed him.

Have you guessed it
my dog's not real
my dog is virtual
he's on my DS.

Matthew McBride (13)
Ifield Community College

My Pet

I asked my father for a pet.
He said, 'I'll take you shopping.'
My father took me to a store
Where animals were hopping.
He asked me, 'Which one would you like?'
So I picked out a puppy,
A parakeet, a rabbit,
Plus a gerbil and a guppy
I also picked a monkey
And a yellow Siamese cat,
A turtle, snake and lizard,
Plus a very big white rat.
My dad said, 'If you want a pet,
Then you will have to feed it.'
Instead, I picked a story book.
I cannot wait to read it.

Axay Shah (13)
Ifield Community College

The Spider

As I tiptoe fearfully along in the dark
What is that pounding?
Is it just my heart?
There is a spider under my brother's bed.
It tore him to shreds . . .
Now he is dead, but his head is still on the bed.
So the bed is stained red.

Charlie Davis (12)
Ifield Community College

Bullies

I'll pound your face
pull your hair
flush your head
without a care.

Beat you down
right to the ground
whack you up
till you fall down.

I'll spit at you
beat you black
beat you blue
graze your face
without a haste.

I hit you with a metal pole
smash your face with no grace
hope you hurt, hope you cry
you can die
for all I care.

You didn't cry, you hurt and died
the ambulance didn't get there in time
they said you smashed the window's glass
hit the ground and got knocked out
you died in a street, cold and wet.

I'm sorry to you.
I beat you up more than I should
I didn't mean for it to go this far
now I stare at life from behind bars.

Charlotte Payne (13)
Ifield Community College

The Sweet Shop

Chocolates are brown
muffins are round
cakes are sweet
and sweets are petite.

Candy is nice
but not with spice
but is with rice
but add no mice.

Lollies are like lorries
they taste so great
but put on a lot of weight
so tell your mate.

Ice has a great gleam
but is really good with cream
and is nice with sauce
but not with a horse.

Adam Harris (12)
Ifield Community College

My Eyes

My brown eyes look upon the blue sky,
Not a fluffy white cloud in sight,
All I can see is a jay bird,
The fresh blue sky,
Nothing left to see,
Except the blue sky.

Chloe Robinson (12)
Ifield Community College

The Secret Lands

One night when I couldn't sleep
Out of my covers I creep,
Down the windy stairs and floors,
Silent in the nightly corridors.

I find a room,
I look around to see some more,
I find a cupboard with an open door,
I decide to go and explore,
Silly, you must think I am,
But the truth is there was a land,
'Amazing!' I said, this must be a dream,
But things aren't always what they seem
Then all of a sudden I heard a scream.

I woke up from my dozy slumber,
And stare at the old wooden beams.
'Phew!' I sighed, what a crazy dream
Then I found myself in the football team.

Startled, dazzled, scared and frightened,
All of a sudden my day was brightened.
I saw myself on my bed,
What was that, am I dead?

Not knowing what was going on,
I wished I was safe and back home,
Started up, looking round,
'Hooray!' I was back, safe and sound.
Dreams can be good, dreams can be scary,
But eventually they just float away like a fairy.

Zimera Veneziani (12)
Ifield Community College

An Abused Child

The bell rings, I sweat,
As I know what approaches me,
The door key turns slowly,
The screechy door opens.

I close my eyes, think happy thoughts,
No matter how hard I try it doesn't go away,
They worm their way back into my thoughts,
I hear the door slam!
My name is shouted,
Why me? What did I do?
They don't care about me,
I was just a mistake.

I hear the footsteps, getting closer and closer,
I can't bear it anymore,
My head is screaming,
1 stroke,
No!
2 stroke,
Help!
3 stroke,
I can't take it anymore,
I am left,
Alone, abandoned,
The tears trickle down my face as I lie there,
Terrified.

Livvy Downing (12)
Ifield Community College

Mystery

The warm chills of this season
running around without a reason.
Kids walk on by, scary but sly
I start to wonder why.
I hear a knock on the door
asking for more,
the chorus of trick or treat
ringing in my head
as though I'm the only one actually sighing.

Guess what season it is?

Luisa Loureiro (12)
Ifield Community College

The Classroom

He was sitting in the classroom listening to the children's whines
But you could see in the teacher's eyes,
                he wanted to break their spines.

Could you really blame him for thinking such nasty thoughts
Because the children were chewing gum
                they really shouldn't have bought?

But as the headmaster walked in, he was shouting at the little devils
But all the headmaster saw was that he was shouting at little angels.

So the teacher packed up all his stuff and said, 'I quit.'
When really he was sacked for shouting at all the kids.

So the reason for this poem is simple 'never mess with kids'
Because they have a way of getting you sacked
                and making you flip your lids.

James Jarman (13)
Ifield Community College

Boys

Boys will be boys,
Shutting you out,
Boys will be boys,
Playing about,
Boys will be boys,
Just keep looking at you.

Boys will be boys,
Just talking about football,
Boys will be boys,
Wrestling,
Boys will be boys,
Just plain old boys.

Tammy Pateman (11)
Ifield Community College

The Fearless Soldiers

We struggle through the mud like an alcoholic,
our clothes ripped and torn.

I need some sleep but I can hear bombs
going off like thunder.

Their boots are covered in mud,
their painful feet covered in blood.
They are like zombies,
their clothes ripped apart
but all I can hear is men screaming with death and fear.

Gas! Put on your gas mask *now*.

I'm panicking, fiddling and struggling with my gas mask,
but one man doesn't make it, he dies in pain.

I can only see green clouds coming towards me
like an evil eagle.

My friend is coming to me slowly,
his eyes falling, his face peeling.
Coughing and choking. I know he is going to die,
I can not help him at all.

This is awful. How would you feel
if you had seen what I've seen?
Your friend dying, his eyes falling and face peeling.

Why would you fight for our country?
Would you be brave or would you be scared?
It's been agony. Do you want glory or agony?

Amber Honisett (13)
Ifield Community College

Who Said You Should Be Proud To Die For Your Country?

Staggering through the damp murky mud,
Rags torn, flooded in blood.

Away from hell, my life they squander,
Bullets and bombs strike like thunder.

Slouching sluggishly with death nearly near,
Bombs landing so distant from my ear,
My feet like bricks pulling me down,
Nothing in sight but soldiers turning brown.

The gas is lurking
The gas is lurking
Stay well clear!

I see death lurking ahead,
A threat of death, a vision through my head,
Scattering for the mask for their face,
The screech of a soldier who can't keep up with the pace

The gas surrounds my short-fixed sight,
Any sudden movement gives everyone a fright

Asking for help the soldier sends me a sign,
How helpless, I feel a shiver down my spine

The soldier pale, with no pulse, no will
The feeling I get for someone to kill,
The useless body rests on my shoulder,
The regrets I have to become a soldier

For your country no need to die,
The fame of war, it's all a lie

Who said you should be proud to die for your country?

Hanzlah Abowath (14)
Ifield Community College

Journey Of Life

Day to day in this pleasant given life,
Some of us get injected with a knife.
Whilst others fly high,
Unfortunate people painfully die.
Why can't you see
The privileges given to ye?
Always look forward and never behind,
As this will only waste precious time.
Treat every heartbeat as the last,
Try and try hard to remove the past.
Never forget to help and lend,
As one day you may also need a friend.

Ashlee Smallwood (13)
Ifield Community College

Friends Forever

F riends forever
R arely apart
I f she was a flower I would pick her
E verlasting friendship
N ever an end
D on't ever break up
S oulmates till the end.

F riends forever
O nly us
R ed as roses
E verlasting bond
V ery special friends
E veryone knows
R eally good friends, love each other loads.

Jessica Pope (13)
Ifield Community College

My Shadow

My shadow always follows me
In the light of day
Until the sun goes down
Then he goes away.

My shadow always follows me
And shrinks towards midday
At evening time he's taller than me
Then at night he goes away.

My shadow always follows me
In the light of day
But at night he can't follow me
He simply fades away.

Charlotte Salmon (13)
Ifield Community College

The Little Girl

Once there was a little girl,
Who always had her hair in curls,
She loved to skip, jump and leap,
Even if her path was steep,
She wouldn't stop working herself all day long,
While she sang her little quiet song,
She loved always having fun,
Even if she had to run,
But one day on the way to school,
She took a trip, a tumble, a fall,
The little girl tried to sit up,
But on her knee was a little cut,
Her eyes started to fill up with water,
Until someone walked by and saw her,
Why are you crying little girl,
With your hair so beautifully curled?
Oh dear you have a cut on your knee,
I'll take you to your mum so she can see,
The little girl was not alone,
As the kind gentle woman took her home,
Her mum cleared up the tiny wound,
And said that it will get better soon,
So she put her trouser leg back down,
And promised that she would be careful now.

Melissa Northcott (13)
Ifield Community College

Space

Up in a rocket I go
Leaving Earth for a while
Passing Saturn, Mars and Pluto.

> A shooting star shot past
> It looked like it was falling from the sky
> As it went really fast.

As Earth got further away
I wondered how far I could go
As I entered the Milky Way.

> I began to feel very sad
> When I looked back to Earth
> As I realised it isn't so bad.

The next thing I knew
I had landed on the moon
Without a clue.

> I didn't want to stay here anymore
> So I set off back to Earth
> My family were waiting at the door.

They said they had missed me
As they gave me a hug
Will I go into space again? Let's wait and see.

Charlotte Hawes (13)
Ifield Community College

School Day

Waking up at 6
Having a nice hot shower
Downstairs for breakfast.

Eating Weetabix
I put my bowl in the sink
Then brushing my teeth.

Out the house by 8
A long hard trek to the school
Going through the door.

To tutor I go,
Meeting my friends on the way
Talking about stuff.

5 lessons we have
Art is my favourite today
The end of the day.

Walking home with friends
Having fun on the way home
Going separate ways.

Melissa Pitts (13)
Ifield Community College

War's War

Staggering through the woods
like a turtle saving his life
swimming through the swamp
with massive army bag that weighs 50 kilos at least
jumping to the ground as bullets fly past you
like a small rocket targeting you
shouting, screaming as yellow gas falls upon you
screaming with fear of choking
while your mates sit there with protection
watching you die a horrible death
drowning inside yourself, dying with honour by the moon
more and more piles on you
while more people die beside you with no honour.
With family and kids crying and sighing
with honour their son or husband wanted to fight
for honour, for their country.
People say it is an honour to die for your country
but all it is, is pain and misery
and a blank dark look before you.

Damien Roberts (13)
Ifield Community College

Death Cloud WWI

As we staggered and tread through thick mud
we are all coughing up blood.

There are mice around my feet
lice in my hair
I am staring back at all the flares.

As we walked away from the death trap
our feet throbbing
there are people behind us who are sobbing
but we are happier because we are leaving death

Gas masks on!

The yellow cloud was in my face
it looked like waste
I managed to get my gas mask on
but my best friend did not
he helped me get mine on
as I was putting his on he moved his head and I dropped it
the cloud came over
as I watched him die
he wanted help that I could not give him
(my hero)

The deadly cloud is thick now
you can hardly hear a sound
you can hear your breathing
we all look scary
but at least we are safer than my friend.

How would you feel if you saw what I saw that day
your friend drowning inside himself
as his lungs filled with all sorts of things
he was fitting, he was in pain
I could not help knowing that it could be me in an hour or two.

If you had the experience that my best friend died
a glorious death
I was told that if we died we would die a nice death!
Yeah right!

Leanna Marshall (13)
Ifield Community College

World Peace

Treading and stepping through thick mud,
Coughing like an old dog.
Behind us, our job done.
We all had dirty old clothes
Jackets like rags,
Trousers like horse blankets and boots like old leather.
So tired they don't even hear gas shells behind them.
Gas! Get out of the way!
Panicking, I put on my mask.
Just in time.
But one poor man dies very slowly.
The gas, like a cloud of yellow smoke,
Moving like a robot in the cloud.
We see him dying horribly,
His face puffed up and his eyes bleeding.
How would you feel if you saw what I saw?

Billy Sansom (13)
Ifield Community College

The Tiger

I was walking alone in a deserted park
And it was pitch-black and very dark.

Then all of a sudden I heard a growl
It sounded like a raging row!

It had black deep depressing eyes
But I promised myself not to cry.

It had black stripes as black as night
Its teeth like daggers, its claws like knives.

It also had ginger stripes and ragged fur
But then all of a sudden I heard a purr.

Then I noticed that the tiger was a girl
And her coat of warmth echoed like a pearl
But then I noticed that she was blind
But she was tame and she was kind.

Then I noticed she had a cub
And against my back it started to rub.

But then I went home and told my mum
She didn't believe me, neither did anyone.
Then I looked out the window and the sun was gleaming
But my mum said that I was just dreaming.

Maxine Smith (11)
Ifield Community College

Pain Is A Mystery

As we walk down the wet, muddy path,
We stomp and stumble over.
We coughed like we were choking on smoke.
I am a smoker but this is bad.
I am one man, one man with a mission.
We reach safety, but leave wandered people behind,
Too tired to help the helpless, even friends, but we save ourselves,
We're not marines, our mission is to save ourselves.
I yawn, the sound of gas shells are blocked out,
Too tired to even feel the burning sensation in our feet.
To be able to feel pain, you need to be alive.
Did I care if I lived or died?

Gas! Save yourselves, do not turn back, don't die.
Do not die. You die then I die. *Run!*
My mask goes over my face.
At that moment nothing else matters but staying alive,
But do I want to stay alive?
I look down and see a boy, a young boy on the floor, not moving,
His eyes are open. But lies like a statue.
Do I want to be in his place?

Breathing heavy and spinning in cycles I don't miss anything in my eyesight.
No sound left but whispered voices in my ears.
I don't know what they are saying.
Are they telling me something?

I grin, would you want to be in the war I came from?
Would you say glorious things after doing the things I did?
Killing people, taking lives, but for what?
A country not even loyal to its own decisions?
Tell me! Do I regret going into war?
   . . . *No,* I wouldn't trade that chance for the world.
I have learnt something about myself.

Jamie Ives (14)
Ifield Community College

Our Love Of The Countryside

I looked at her like a shimmering river
Reflected by the boiling beams of the sun.
The times we spent together loved and loved
As the unbreakable one.

The first time I met her was in the village of love.
Where together we looked at the stars above.

The love I shared with her was magical and cool.
I promised her one thing, I would never be a fool.

The passion we shared was together every night.
So we looked up at the stars that were shining so bright.

I vowed never to hurt her and I never will.
But there is something inside me wanting me to kill.

The morning came, there was no doubt about that.
But we now have a child who is sort of a brat.

I love her so dearly I will never leave her or go away.
The love we share I love each day.

I look at her eyes, loving her too much.
Her smile is magical and brilliant as such.

We respect and love one another.
I can't stop talking about her to my big, big brother.

Love is dear, love is might.
I'm glad to be with her each and every night.

We love each other dearly, no one can stop us now.
The love we share is brilliant like the night sky wolf howl.

Our children have grown up as have we too.
But the love is right there, it's just beside you.

So love is everywhere, anyone can find it.
Or love will find you, no point having a fit.

I found love and I am happy.
So treasure on to her because she is so lovely.

Jamie Keay (14)
Ifield Community College

Dead Or Alive

As we drag swollen feet, we cough like old smokers.
As we walk the bombs shoot ahead where the rest awaits.
My shoes with holes as if a rodent has made a home in them,
while my shirt, tatty like the tramp next to me.
As the bomb shells are getting closer by the minute.

Gas attack!

I help myself to the gas masks,
When I look behind me I see a man who awaits death.
I see the cloud of death, following me,
slower than a leg with gangrene.
The face of Satan confronts me as I walk,
with his eyes oozing with pus.

What would you do if you had to walk behind the wagon?
How would you feel if you saw a friend die?
Nothing left but an empty shell.

Every night is the same, people dying, people crying.
Living each day like there was no tomorrow.

Pritesh Wadher (14)
Ifield Community College

War Poem

As we trudged and stomped through the trenches
we coughed and belched as we walked away
we left the bursting shells and the frantic flares behind us
we dared not look back at our rat-infested dump.

We looked like our energy had been sucked out by a straw
and the men looked like they'd just been to a funeral
we had cuts, bruises, scratches and burns.
We had no hope of seeing our kids.
Gas!

We hurried like birds escaping from gunshots
we all successfully got our gas masks on but one man.
He looked like he was drowning.

The gas was like a plague emerging from Hell
I could not see my comrades through the foggy fracas.

I was looking for my comrade and I saw my friend
coughing and spluttering.
I stared helplessly at him.

How would you feel watching your friend dying in agony?
The feeling in my stomach was like I'd been shot.
How would you feel if you had to carry him to a truck?

I was not a hero, you lied, my friend did not die a glorious death,
he was not a hero.

Aaron Finch (13)
Ifield Community College

First World War Poem

Soon will be falling, like the ground is eating us alive.
Coughing and heaving, our blood dripping down our English badges
as we wear them with pride.
As I limp towards shelter all I can hear is bombs and screaming
as my feet dig deeper and deeper into the diseased mud.
The men all falling, lower each time,
the tattered and torn boots as the feet forced to move,
staggering into the fog, I can hear little tapping noises of gas bombs,
I did not turn around as I feared the sight.
Get out of the way! Put your gas masks on. Hurry, no time to cry!
Oh no, I can't find the mask.
Behind me the gas is coming nearer and nearer.
I put the mask on, behind the death trap is storming after me,
I turn as the gas rushes through my body.
I shiver, there's a man too slow,
I watched in devastation as he choked,
his chest bursting in slow motion.
All I can see is fog, yellowish pea colour like soup,
rushing around in a circle, I can hear my comrades
but I can't see them, as I turn and
see a flea nest in my pocket.
Suddenly my friend comes staggering
his blood covering the plastic over my eyes, I want to help
but now crying in agony, I turn the other way to help.
How would you feel huh? I can still hear his voice,
him coughing in the back of the truck
as I watched him struggling to catch his breath.
I can't even imagine the pain, the fear, could you?
You all lied to me, you all did!
Fighting for my country, it was not glorious,
you would never be happy, never,
my children never question me about the war, I hate you all.
I have no pride.

Hajra Jameel (13)
Ifield Community College

The End Of The World

They were coughing and sneezing as they trudged through the mud.
As they walked away I could hear the bombs blasting
but they seemed closer then ever then.
Suddenly I walked away panicking.

They moved, they could not give up.
They were so tired as they moved.
They did not even care if they had muddy feet
or lost their boots.

'Everyone move, the gas is coming!
Move, move, move!'

One is too slow and cries out as the gas enters his lungs.
He did not do anything but tried to get his gas mask on
but he could not, he gave up but then he tried again for his own life.
But then he was panicking as he slowly slipped away.

You couldn't see as you slowly woke up,
then you saw a pea soup colour you thought *what is happening, is this
a silly dream that I've thought of again?*

You felt totally helpless, the coughing is horrible
and you knew he was going to die.

I went over to him and said, 'Are you alright my friend?'
He did not answer, he was totally lost and me as well.

He was dying as he tried to lay down.
I felt tired and helpless but I didn't know what to do.

I wanted to help everyone but they suddenly died
and then I felt that I would be the next one to die.

It is not good to die for your country,
for something that you have not done, that have not done wrong.
'We did not do anything to them Germans.
I am saying this because I am fed up of this,
I now feel that I am slowly dying.'

Everyone thought that we were the big guys,
we can do it for our country.
We could beat the Germans and win and try hard but now, how now!
It is the end of the world!

Humail Hussain (13)
Ifield Community College

The Dead Men

Me and my comrades are stomping through the soggy mouldy mud.
We were coughing up blood like we had cancer.
As we fell back the noise of the golden shells faded
                              with the dead soldiers' bodies.
We lost our boots, some lost their lives.
As we got closer to the prey thinking they could die too
while getting cut by the used shells as they fell and fell,
cutting, cutting down in numbers.
Hoping they know what they're getting into.
Heads up, gas! As we shoved the gas masks on I saw one of us,
fade away with the mustard gas like a leaf in the wind.
I stood still waiting for the smoke to clear.
I was gasping to see my comrades as the sounds of the shell shots.
As I saw my comrades rushing through to the enemy
I knew I wouldn't see them again.
I could see the blood and the men dying.
How would you feel if you saw your family dying one by one,
you hoping they're not dead?
Would you still say it is a glorious way to die for your country?
No, I don't think you would.

Kamran Asif (13)
Ifield Community College

Death's Door

There I was
Walking and coughing,
And slowly sinking into the cold wet mud,
As we march for safety in front of us we can see a peaceful lane,
But behind us is the battle claiming more victims.
The exploding bombs terrify us as well as the crackle of gunfire.

'Gas!' I heard someone repeatedly shout.
We all tried to put on our gas masks as fast as we could.
But one of us was not so fortunate. He ran to me, gasping for breath
And holding onto my leg for dear life, I felt so helpless.
In the gas mask I could hear my breath and my heartbeat racing.
All I could see was the huge yellow smog of mustard gas,
I could see soldiers dying, like a fly being sprayed with bug killer.
Seeing the bodies lying there like mimes from Hell
Was the worst I had ever felt in my life.

How would you feel following the wagon of your dead soldiers?
They did not die a glorious death, it was slow and painful.
There is no point fighting.
They didn't die for fame, they died in horrific pain.

Krisjan Boddy (14)
Ifield Community College

The Deadly War

Staggering through the mud as if I were in quicksand.
Coughing like an old hag.

Marching away from the battle but I know that there's people dying
every second and I desperately want to help them.

The men are so tired that they desperately need rest,
they can just see our ship but there's torn, tatty clothes
through the squelching mud, boots like bricks,
heavy as I carry them.

'Gas! Quick men!'

I can't get the bloody thing on, we all get them on in time,
I notice a lad that can't get his on his face, trembling with fear.

The gas is a thick cloud of death, I hear nothing.

I see nothing but gas, then suddenly a man jumps out
and grabs onto my face for dear life,
pleading for me to help him,
he has no mask on and his bulging eyes stare into mine
with great hate.

How would you feel if you had to put a lifeless man
onto the wagon of death?
His life was drained out of him.

If you weren't there, there is no way you should go there.

There was a man dying,
knowing that he would never see his wife and kids again.

Sam Rutter (14)
Ifield Community College

The Glory Of Death

Stamping heavily in the mud like a herd of elephants,
coughing like there had only been little air left around me.
Walking back I could hear the faint sounds of screams,
whizzes and bullets spreading across the land.

The lads and I looked as though we have been pushed
into a shredder; our torn tatty clothes hanging onto our bodies.
Sounds have faded but death is still falling behind me
and every man here today.

The fearful poisonous gas sprayed us like a kid using bug spray
on an insect. We were the insects this time.

'Gas! Run men run! Quick get out now!'

Panic and fear fell over my body
as I tried to put on the gas mask as quickly as I could.
Silence. My heart beat faster and faster,
a greenish sick-like gas covers my view of everything
                              like a bedcover.

Moments later I was being pushed and grabbed,
a comrade dying in front of me, coughing and spitting like mad
as he tried to get air, hands round his neck as his eyes popped out,
looking like the Devil from Hell.

How would you feel if one of your comrades grabbed you
for your help and there was nothing you could do?
Looking like just bones and skin was left,
coughing loud like an engine starting.

Becoming a hero for your country, yeah right. Die in glory,
more like die in pain and deadly surroundings. It's all a lie.

Danielle Johnson (14)
Ifield Community College

The Glorious War Of Death And Deceit

I can hardly walk, my feet like a dying dog
as we cough like I am in a city of smoke and death.
Miraculously marching back to the ship,
hearing the endless screams of the lifeless.
My clothes are all ripped and sliced
and my boots are dissolving away into my feet.
I can hardly hear the banging and the dropping of the bombs near,
all I can hear and feel is pain.
'Gas! Everybody, down, move, fast move.'
It's awkward, how do you do it?
Help, no save yourself, I have done it, have you?
Where's your mask?
All I can see is the greenish smoke which looks
so safe and comfy but deadly.
I can't see anything, just this cloud of death coming towards me,
my heart beating as fast as it can,
the only thing that can now keep me alive and safe.
All I can see is the greenish cloud
and suddenly he appears out of nowhere,
dying in front of me.
I don't know what to do with his bulging eyes and greyish face.
How would you feel? Yeah you,
if you had to pull the wagon with a man dying,
twitching, having fits in the every possible way
with his bulging eyes, and greyish face
with the lungs that he no longer has and will never get back.
If you were in this war you wouldn't be able to cope
with the glory that is not true.
They lie, in the posters you see, never trust them,
you don't feel like a hero, you feel like a zero and you never will.
Don't be fooled.

Ashlee Saward (11)
Ifield Community College

The Ghost Ship

There was a captain of a ghost ship
And the ship would sway and tip
He heard a bang
As he bit an apple with his fang.

The boat crashed
And the lighthouse flashed
The villagers came
But all they wanted was fame.

The boat disappeared
And everybody feared.

Adam Lambert (11)
Ifield Community College

The Sea

The waves roar on the beach.
The waves crash and boom on the cliff.
The seas smash the boats.
Down below a blue whale merrily sleeps on the seabed.
I like the sea and the waves going whoosh.

John Bye (11)
Ifield Community College

Once Upon A Time

Once upon a time, far, far away,
a mouse said to a big fat ogre,
'How are you today?'

Once upon a time, in a faraway land,
an ogre smiled at a mouse
and shook his little hand.

Once upon a time, in a faraway place,
the mouse challenged an ogre,
the ogre to a race.

'I will win,' said the ogre, 'for I am as tall as a tree.'
'No, I will win,' said the mouse, 'just watch me.'

And so the ogre and the mouse,
competed in a race,
once upon a time, long, long ago,
in a merry little place.

After the race (the mouse had won for he was very fast),
the ogre said (he was out of breath),
'I know that I came last.'

The mouse felt sorry for the ogre,
and gave his head a little bend.
He gave the ogre his tiny trophy and said,
'Come on, let's be friends.'

Anna Fraser (11)
Ifield Community College

A Parrot In A Cage

The parrot was awoken
from where he was taken
further and further he went
he did not know what this meant.

He long dreamt of when he shall flee
this reminded him of when he was free.

As the time went by
he began to cry.
He was no longer wanted
and his cage became haunted.

'I'll take him for 99p.'
'It does not matter, take him for free.'
The lady once thought how cruel it would be
if she was taken from her family.

She opened the cage
he filled with rage.
But then he began to flee,
he started to think he was finally free.

Chloe Langley (12)
Ifield Community College

Football

When I walk on the football ground,
My love for football is suddenly found.

I kick the ball for the first time,
Then football snatches my mind.

When I get fouled,
The crowd hisses and howls.

I score a great goal,
When I hit it with all my soul.

The final whistle blows,
Then all the crowd goes.

We walk off the pitch and through the tunnel
Then we all form a huge muddle.

Craig Nichols (11)
Ifield Community College

The Jungle Flu

Birds singing
Raindrops dripping
Hear the wild roar
See the monkeys in the tree
Hear the lion, you don't want to see
But when it comes to going home
To see your TV and your phone
But no
You don't want to go
Because you have caught the jungle flu.

Jack Munday (11)
Ifield Community College

The Girl

She walks along the corridors
She jumps up the stairs
She stares at all the girls
Who show off their underwear.

When there is a test
She never has to correct
But even though she's the cleverest
Everyone else is a pest!

Rebecca Denne (11)
Ifield Community College

Skateboarding

Skateboarders can grind
Scratching up the paths
Skateboarders can combo
Improving their new tricks
Skateboarders can do 360
Moving through the half pipes
Skateboarders can do the *melody*
That's cool
The new tricks you gain
The more skateboarding pain
Come on let's skate.

Sade Rushton (11)
Ifield Community College

Graffiti

Graffiti is not a crime
So why are we doing time?

It's simply just an art
From deep within the heart.

For graffiti is something really smart
It's as tangy as a lemon tart.

So when you walk by, don't think *oh them kids*
Think . . . *wow! that's from those kids!*

Graffiti is not a crime
So why are we doing time?

Danny Ellery (11)
Ifield Community College

Four Friends

My friend Mollie,
Is such a dolly,
She plays with her hair and phone,
She is my best friend,
So I'm never alone.

My friend Joe,
Well he never goes,
He's always there for me,
He is a good friend,
And we will always be.

My friend George,
Is never bored,
He is never horrible at all,
He is a good person, someone to look up to,
Plus he is really tall.

But then there's me
The fourth person, Chloe,
I'm the loud mouth but proud
I like to be cheeky
Just like Mollie,
Only if we're allowed.

Us friends have problems,
But we solve them,
We are the best of friends
And that will never end.

Chloe Hill (11)
Ifield Community College

Dragons

Dragons, dragons everywhere,
Everything glowing with its flare.

People screaming, people shout,
People running inside out.

Dragons, dragons everywhere,
Everything glowing with its flare.

People murdered, people dead,
Everything is unexpected.

Dragons, dragons everywhere,
Everything glowing with its glare.

The dragons are gone, everything ash,
Everything seems just like a flash.

George Thorne (12)
Ifield Community College

I Hate School

School is dull and boring,
It makes me feel like snoring.
School I don't like,
Because you have to write all night.
School is for muppets,
They use you like puppets.
I hate school,
It's the worst thing of all.

Sitting at home all alone,
Would be better than seeing a teacher,
Sitting on a throne.
I hate school,
It makes me feel like a fool.

Thomas Montague-Tompson (11)
Ifield Community College

Gruesome Gas

I and my brothers are sitting in our moth-eaten beds
cleaning our weapons of mass destruction.
The cause of most of the pain.
We sat there as the rats ran about us, as they ran out
of the rotting carcasses of my brothers and my enemies.
We start to march from the front line,
hopefully to get back to the trench in time.
As we leave the bomb shells,
rotting carcasses and the flares of battle behind me thankfully.
My brothers are too tired to walk as they staggered like
drunken men coming out of the pub, they wheeze like old hags.
Some of them are limping
as the painful cuts make walking impossible.
All of a sudden we hear the Devil's choir singing the song of death,
we turn around, the gas bombs are flying in towards us.
We panic, I shout out, 'Gas masks on!'
The fiddly life savers were our only chance to save our lives,
so we can see our beautiful wives
who are waiting for the dreadful call,
saying that we had been taken victim of the war.
My brothers fiddled with the gas masks,
as we watched the sea of death.
I saw one of my brothers struggling with his mask,
he was panicking like a child that knew
that he had done something wrong.
There was nothing I could do
as the choking blanket smothered him in a most alarming manner.
He collapsed to his knees, drowning in his own blood
as it came frothing up to his mouth, making a gurgling noise.
He looks like a dog with rabies.
There was nothing I could do, there was nothing I could do . . .

Joseph Maynard (14)
Ifield Community College

My Midnight Cats

The moon was shining brightly
above the stormy seas
the trees were waving gently
into the evening breeze
the daytime creatures were moving
into their nice warm beds
and my midnight cats were flying,
flying,
flying,
my midnight cats were flying
around the moonlit sky.

They all had short black fur
and glowing, gleaming eyes
they all had a carefree spirit
and wonderful wings to fly
they all had small sharp teeth
and lovely gentle purrs
and my midnight cats were flying,
flying,
flying,
my midnight cats were flying
around the moonlit sky.

No more will see my cats
no one will at all
only when in danger
do they cry their cat call
so never will you see them
dancing around your heads
but my midnight cats are flying,
flying,
flying,
my midnight cats are flying
around the moonlit sky.

Claudia-Rose Spears (13)
Ifield Community College

What Is Love?

Love is when two people care about each other.
Love can be a strange thing
but loving is what keeps me knowing that I'm with you.
Love is me and you together forever.
Love is when I go to sleep knowing we love each other.
So what do you think love is?

Jade Powis (13)
Ifield Community College

Carrots

Carrots are orange and pointy.
They are grown in the ground
And are found brown and dirty.

They can be used for anything,
In a stew or for your rabbit.

A farmer picks a weed and plants a seed
Three weeks later the seed is done,
The carrot is made in a carrot bun.

Jamie Bridle (13)
Ifield Community College

A Cricket Poem

Daniel came out to the crease.
He started to get pretty teased,
he swung his bat,
like he would ever do that,
and that was that,
and the team was in misery.

Crawley came out to bowl.
The batsmen all got told.
The last man came in,
he played himself in.
He got his fifty,
that was pretty nifty.

The last ball of the day,
always fun to play,
hit the wicket,
just like taking a ticket,
now the other team were in disgrace.

Adam Dallamore (13)
Ifield Community College

Say My Name

Don't forget me because I'm still in your thoughts
I may not be here in person but I will always watch over you,
guide you through your years.
Remember to look up at me so I know you still care.
Because I am your sister, that's why I care.
My name means everything,
so please don't stop talking about me
as long as it's all good.
Remember the good times we spent together
but don't remember the bad.
I don't think there was any bad
because we love each other so much.
Our mum doesn't talk about you anymore
I'm really sorry but in my dreams, I talk to you,
I have the ring as a sign you are still with me
inside my heart, inside my soul.

Well sister, together forever, me and you.

Cheryl Bryant-Owens (14)
Ifield Community College

A Cricket Poem

The captains went out to do the toss
One captain lost and got very cross
The openers went out to bat
They put on their hat
The bowler marked out his mark
The batsman hit the ball out of the park
He got his fifty
And the crowd thought it was pretty nifty.

Daniel Burt (13)
Ifield Community College

Day And Night

The sun is big, the sun is tall
It glows as bright as a fireball
But when the day goes and turns to night
You will get a massive fright
Because monsters see food in their sight at night
As the monsters come out to feed
Be careful because they like to greed
And as they greed they like to fight
Under the moon of the starry night.

Arron Hall (13)
Ifield Community College

On The Way To Grandma's House

On the way to Grandma's house
I like to stop and stare.
On the way to Grandma's house
we smell the cold sweet air.
On the way to Grandma's house
we follow the long stony trail.
On the way to Grandma's house
it begins to hail.
On the way to Grandma's house
we feel the refreshing rain.
On the way to Grandma's house
we see it trickle down the drain.
On the way to Grandma's house
we knock on the door.
On the way to Grandma's house
we all sleep on her comfy floor!

Caine Hawkins (13)
Ifield Community College

My Life

My life is filled with dreams and hope
But I'm so confused
I cannot cope.

Will they happen, will I fail?
Will my dreams
Fall like hail?

I dream to be a TV star,
Be rich and own
A sporty car.

But what if I'm to fail my dream?
I could try to be in
A football team.

Yeah, that's it, that would be cool,
But only if I
Could hit the ball!

Who knows how my life will go?
But I'll be calm
And go with the flow.

Ben Logan (13)
Ifield Community College

Nature

Nature's green
Nature's brown
Nature's blue
And all around the town.

Nature's kind
Nature's here
So why don't you
Just give a cheer.

Thank you Nature
For being kind
And thank you Nature
For keeping me alive!

Krystal Nichols (13)
Ifield Community College

Bats

They are dark,
They are spooky,
They are always invisible.

They are black,
Their wings are flat,
It is a bat.

They fly in the dark,
They feed on pollen
And suck on blood.

They don't like light,
But they like dark,
And they will come for you and bite.

Won't they die?
Won't they live?
They will always be evil.

Phillip Hibbert (13)
Ifield Community College

Snow

It is cold outside
and now there's snow
all the squirrels need to hide
and now it's night all the stars glow.

Now out comes the morning sun
all the snow has dried up
but now the sun has done
the snow is now water in a cup.

Billy Whinder (13)
Ifield Community College

School

When you're sitting at your desk
with nothing to do
then you have just realised
you've got bubblegum on your shoe.

You forgot to do your homework
and it's due in today
and the teacher says, 'What have you done?'
and I said, 'Oops, I threw it away!'

Chloe Cooke (11)
Ifield Community College

Birds

Birds fly,
up so high,
their wings are gliding,
when they're riding,
they look like planes,
swooping down.

Emily Sidhom (11)
Ifield Community College

Words

W onderful wicked words,
O utrageous and amazing spellings,
R idiculous abbreviations,
D evastating description,
S uper sentences filled with words,
   they're all around us, just have a look.

Jason Harrold (11)
Ifield Community College

Cars

Wheels turning, tyres screaming,
Engine roaring, petrol restoring,
Gear shifting, speed lifting,
All of this could end quite soon,
With you wrapped round a tree like a spoon.

Gary Sawyer (12)
Ifield Community College

Monkey

M is for mischievous,
O is for outrageous,
N is for naughty,
K is for kooky,
E is for energetic,
Y is for yappy.

Rebecca Wilde (11)
Ifield Community College

Ferdinand

F erdinand
E xcellent
R isky
D ynamic
I ntelligent
N imble
A gile
N atural
D aring.

William McKnight
Ifield Community College

The Day That I Lived

As we trudge through the thick mud,
we're coughing and spitting as we're looking at blood.

There's lice in our clothes and our boots are not there
and we can see all the flares.

As I walk away I can still hear the bomb behind me ringing in my ear.
My feet are all cut and my friends are not.

'Look, put your gas mask on quick!'

The cloud is right there, and I'm so scared,
we're all in a hurry but Tom's too slow
he's crying out as he drowns.

The gas is so thick and as green as pea soup.
Tom was dying and I knew I couldn't help.

Would you like to feel the way I did that day
I saw my best mate die?

It was all lies and I wanted to say,
It's not the best time of your life!

Cassandra Killner (14)
Ifield Community College

The Terrible Truth Of The War

I can hardly walk, my feet dragging like the dead,
coughing and spluttering as if I have been trapped
in a room of smoke and the undying tension of death.

Morbidly marching back to the ship of the dead,
hearing the deafening screams of the lifeless
waiting for their time to come.

The dark dreary grey faces like the dead staring at me
with no feelings, marching slowly back to the ship
most with no boots, many with trench foot, hearing the men cry
with fear in their screams, everything so peaceful,
not even able to hear the sound of the dreaded gas shells
falling fast behind us.

'Run lads run, unless you want to die, move it, move it!'

Seeing the green gas surging towards us
waiting for our deaths, everyone rushing like a pack of wild animals,
one lad, no mask, and the worst is still to happen.

I can no longer hear, only a muffled sound rings through my ears,
the gas reaching out, trying to clench us,
hearing my own heart beat faster and faster.

Struggling through the thick blanket of death,
someone grabs me, holding onto me tight,
I turn round fast, he is hideous, hearing him screaming
in my mouth and coughing heavily,
he looks like something from my nightmares,
bulging eyes, face deathly.

Could you imagine pulling your friend in the wagon
to the hospital where their fate lies, knowing they may die?
How would you feel looking into the face of death?
How would you feel seeing an innocent soul dying in front of you?

You know how all those posters and people in the streets tell you
it would be great to die for your country, well guess what,
it isn't, we all got tricked into thinking.
All those innocent people died, don't let yourself be tricked too.

Emma Wiltshire (14)
Ifield Community College

Gas Attack

As we stagger through the thick mud like a drunk man
and coughing up blood like a waterfall
we walk to safety, bits of mud and stones flying inches past you,
and our ears yelling like they are going to pop.
We walk away from demolished grounds and trees,
looking back, just to make sure gas hasn't been set off.
Some men in front of me with gashes out of their legs and feet,
some of them with only one boot on.

We forget to look back because we are so tired
 and gas has gone off,
I shout out to the men, 'Gas masks, gas masks, hurry up! Gas!'
We quickly put our gas masks on,
it's like swimming through a load of gas,
I look through a little plastic bit in the gas masks
and see a man crying out, 'Help! Help! Please!'
As he falls to the ground the gas is so thick now I can't see anything,
I close my eyes hoping it is all a dream,
but when I open them, no it isn't,
I look around like a robot.

His face was like a drowning cat, as he runs over to me
with his hands round his neck coughing.

How would you feel if you were watching your friend being gased?
Could you?
Your friend sitting in the back of a truck.
It's not true, all the things I've been told.
'It's glorious to die for your country, all the girls will love you'.
That person didn't die a glorious death.

Josh Reeve (13)
Ifield Community College

Politically Incorrect

Cats will take over the Earth,
Vegetarians should be put down,
England is the only country worth living in.

I know it,
You know it,
We both know it,
You just won't admit it.

Younger sisters should be put in an asylum,
Sports day is all about winning,
Children should watch Disney films as part of their education.

I know it,
You know it,
We both know it,
You just won't admit it.

Old people should be banned from insulting 'youth today',
'Technical difficulties' on aeroplanes should be made illegal,
People who talk to animals need to be locked up.

I know it,
You know it,
We both know it,
You just won't admit it.

Ana-Maria Braddock (13)
Millais School

Frogs

What could be more perfect than a frog?
Hopping around all day without a care in the world
In and out of the water
It doesn't care so long as it can hop.

What could be more perfect than a frog?
All sorts of colours, some for a warning
Some for camouflage,
And some just for the fun of colours.

What could be more perfect than a frog?
A smile up to its big love-filled eyes
Little sticky balls for toes
So small you can hold it in one hand.

What could be more perfect than a frog?
All it wants to do is send you a smile
Make you happy all day long
Just to be your best friend.

What could be more perfect than a frog?
Nothing,
Nothing in the whole world
Could be more perfect than a frog.

Nicky Blyth (13)
Millais School

Away With The Fairies

The rain falls down, patter, patter, all around
Out I run, my socks are soaked
To find my fairy people.
They dance and prance, their wings fluttering too fast to see,
But luckily for me I can imagine their faces - round, sweet, full of joy
Of being allowed to play with me - so I play.
They show me secret paths to other worlds,
They show me their village, hidden by trees,
A magical rock, a sacred den, around a hill and back again.

Wading up the winding stream,
Avoiding the monsters, especially the big red one,
Full of people he has eaten,
Then - out pops the sun, and that is it, my fun is over
Till my fairy friends come back.

But one day,
They never came.
The rain fell down, patter, patter all around
Out I ran, my socks were soaked,
But - that's it
All I saw was just rain
Just water falling from the sky - just water,
Falling onto mud - just mud.

I walked up my winding street,
Avoiding the cars, especially the big red bus,
Full of people from work.
Why couldn't I see them? Where had they gone?
And then I realised
Not they had gone, but I.
I had grown up, away and left them behind,
So now my imagination has gone, gone,
Away with the fairies.

Natasha Foote (13)
Millais School

Horse Feeling

Wind rushing past my face,
Hooves pounding on the ground,
Strides lengthening, speed increasing,
Cantering towards the exciting gallop,
Kicking on, going faster,
Her tail swishing, her ears pricked,
Shortening up the reins,
Preparing for the final hurdle,
We jump clearly,
The noise from the crowd is eerily loud,
I receive my rosette, I came in first.
What a feeling,
What a feeling.

Heidi Forster (13)
Millais School

A Smile For You

Sometimes when I smile I'm as happy as can be,
A smile from my bestest friend may bring back memories,
A smile from a friend or peer is worth just so much more,
Than shoes and clothes and diamond rings
                           from all the high street stores,
A smile can be true or false, it's not that hard to tell,
If it's painted on or if it's true you know that they mean well,
My friend gave me a smile today as she was passing by,
She used no words or gestures but I knew that she meant 'Hi',
That's the thing with smiles you see, you've got to look inside,
You know that there's a meaning there, but it ran away to hide,

Smiling straight at someone else can make you feel so good,
For if you didn't smile at them today in class, who would?
You never know you may receive another smile back,
And then you know they understood and sure to be
                                       on the right track,
Smiles are infectious and you might catch one yourself,
To pass it on you show your teeth and open up your mouth,
This is how you spread the joy so far and yet so fast,
Before you know it might have travelled right around the class,

So next time when you smile just remember it's a pleasure,
To understand the meaning of a smile you can't measure,
It's sent to you, you pass it on for mile after mile,
But just make sure that every day you give your friend a smile . . .

Jessica Langan (13)
Millais School

Boredom

Even being bored is getting boring now
Trying to find something to do, but how?
The games in my cupboard have all been played
And my notebooks are full of scribbles
And have seen better days
The books on my shelves are torn and tattered
And my CD player has become quite battered
The computer that's on my desk is old and slow
And my iPod's on the blink and so's my mobile phone
The garden's thick with mud and there's puddles outside too
And the karaoke machine's broken, the microphone's
                                        snapped in two
My brother's on the PlayStation, confined to his room
And my mum's in the kitchen, singing to some old tune
Bored to death I sit on my bedroom floor
Trying to figure out how I can be bored no more
When I'm bored with thinking of all these different ways
I spot that bit of homework I've been putting off all day!

Siân Ward (13)
Millais School

Pets

I have many pets,
big ones, small ones,
soft ones, cuddly ones,
I have many pets,
I have four hamsters, Patch, Toffee, Teeny and Weenie,
Teeny and Weenie like to squeak,
they run very fast, jump and leap,
all Toffee and Patch do is sleep,
I have many pets.
I have three rabbits,
their names are Chocolate, Jake and Nina,
they are all very sweet,
they like to claw things and gnaw things,
they each go through six bowls of food a week,
basically all they do is eat,
last but not least, I have ten stick insects,
I have had them for four months now,
the word I would use to describe them is 'wow'
they are amazing little creatures and funny to watch,
I love all my pets dearly and love them a lot!

Hannah Wright (13)
Millais School

Three Troublesome Brothers

First there's Alex, born to argue,
One day soon, I'm sure I'll gag you!
Good at football, any sport in fact,
Especially the ones with a strong impact.
Loves to play games and his PS2,
But hates to do chores and have homework to do.

Next it's Oli, who's a bit like me,
Very lazy and creative and loves to be free.
Often has friends 'round, which we all find unfair,
And just so you know, that's an absolute nightmare!
Always starts an argument, and then gets us into trouble,
And then teases Max, who's his absolute double!

Lastly it's Max, the clown of the house,
Who entertains most, and loves the woodlouse.
He will never shut up and always chatters,
And goes through life like nothing matters.
He loves to go golfing and wants to be seen,
But doesn't understand: a driver on the putting green?

My brothers are troublemakers, and that's what I see,
But without them here, where would I be?

Abigail High (13)
Millais School

I Sing Silent Prayers

I sing silent prayers,
To a star peaked sky,
Whisper words of comfort,
To a world that rushes by,
Not long now till morning,
Life comes with dawn,
So I'll use my time wisely,
Drown in darkness until morn,
I'll whisper gentle curses,
To a dusty night sky,
I'll recite sweet poem verses,
To the comfort of the night.

I sing silent prayers,
As the world goes on by,
Whisper words of knowledge,
In darkness I'm not shy,
In night there are no eyes,
Piercing your skin,
In darkness you can open,
To the world we're living in,
Escape the day,
Receive the night,
Ignore what others say,
Yes, I'll sing silent prayers,
To that which comes before day.

Charlotte Keegan (13)
Millais School

Life

When you're five,
You want to be six,
Then seven,
Then eight.

Just wishing your life away,
And it's not until you're old,
That you finally realise,
You're fine just the way you are.

Then it's too late,
You're at Heaven's gate,
There's no turning back,
Because of the mistakes.

Ashes to ashes,
Dust to dust,
That's why remember,
Enjoy it you must.

Lydia Churcher (13)
Millais School

My Family

My family is full of madness
I see it every day
Though this may seem quite funny
I'd have it no other way.

My dad is singing as loud as he can
Mum begins to moan
Because amongst all the noise
She was trying to talk on the phone.

My brother gets really embarrassed
Though he acts like he doesn't care
But when my aunties say weird things
He looks away in despair.

Grandma has lost her glasses
Grandpa has fallen asleep
I hope it's not because of our company
Which he's having to keep.

My great grandma is obsessed with the news
She soaks up every word
And then she bores my mum to death
With the stories that she's heard.

So when I think of family
However strange they may be
Without them there and all their fun
I guess I wouldn't be me!

Phoebe Hodges (14)
Millais School

Tennis

One to a side or maybe two,
Tennis players are very few.
But all those who play the game,
Use their racquets and achieve fame.

Learning tennis is not so tough,
But at first you might pant and puff.
Fitness is what this game wants,
Doesn't matter if you haven't played in yonks!

Playing tennis is loads of fun,
But it takes time to learn.
If you spend your time playing tennis,
It could take you to America, Paris or Venice.

Losing a game is no big deal,
However upset you may feel.
So friend, hear my advice,
Make learning tennis your first choice.

Lucy Ford (13)
Millais School

My Bedroom

If you go in my bedroom then you will see
Everything that makes my identity
Over the years your bedroom may change
To suit your personality, however strange
When you are young you have toys everywhere
As you get older you just don't seem to care
Sometimes your parents may influence you
May paint your walls and buy pictures too
But whatever happens it's somewhere to go
It's something for you to call your own.

Emily Colson (13)
Millais School

Growing Up/Teddy

Identity's like a teddy
to go with you everywhere
you cling to it when you are frightened
and feeling a little despaired
you don't know why or how
but it comforts you quite a lot
you've had it since you were a baby
sleeping in your cot
your family and friends are growing
distant by the day
soon it's only you
and your teddy left to play
then one morning you wake up and
cannot seem to find,
your teddy, your identity
you search all through your mind
now you've lost your teddy
your friends and family too
now you've done it
now you've lost the thing
that makes you 'you'.

Georgina Russell (14)
Millais School

Netball

Netball is really great to play
I could play it every day
Goal attack is my favourite position,
And when I play it I am on a mission
A mission to win, a mission to be ace,
And others really can't stand the pace
So as I said before, I love netball; it's great,
It's gym and dance I really hate!

Emma Brown (13)
Millais School

New School

N ever-ending days of work,
E xciting making new friends,
W orrying about how I am going to fit in.

S cary meeting new teachers in a big school
C ruel bullies scaring me in the playground,
H oping the day will go great.
O nly me in this big world,
O rganising homework for the next day,
L onely at break time when no one's there for me.

Elizabeth Duebel (11)
Millais School

A Way With My Animals

M uddy
Y oung

D igging
O ptimistic
G rowly.

G orgeous
E njoyable
M onkey
M oody
A untie.

C uddly
A crobatic
T ails
S weet.

P ast
O mega
L oud
O nce.

R acy
A nti-fight
G angs
S oft.

F un
I mportant
S elfish
H andful.

Animals are so fun.

Chloe Hunt (11)
Millais School

Great I'm A Celebrity

Great, great, great!
I walk into a shop.
Great, great, great!
Oh no I forgot!
I'm a celebrity, what do I do?

I walk into a piece of poo
Great, great, great!
The paparazzi came out, what do I do?
They ask me things
They bring me things.

Ahh what do I do?

I go into another shop
Great, great, great!
They all come in
I try to hide in a dustbin
Great, great, great!

The bin tips over
What do I do?
I want to get out
I wanna shout
Great, great, great!

What do I do?
I hate it
I hate being a celebrity
I hate paparazzi
I hate it
Great, great, great!
What do I do?

I want to wake up
To see if it's real
But no I am, it's a big deal
All because I'm a . . .
Celebrity!

Tamsin Romain (12)
Millais School

Homeless Person

I wish I was not poor
But I wish not too rich
All I would ask is to have a home

I beg each day
For food, water
Just something to keep me alive.
How else would I survive?

I cry
Because I'm lonely
All I would ask is to have a cuddle
I wish I had a mum.

I shiver night and day
I am so cold
Not just outside but in too.
I feel all alone
Although I know there are thousands like me

I just want a home!

Charlotte Roadley (11)
Millais School

A Present For Christmas

Here I am wrapped up in a parcel.
It's stuffy in here and very dark,
All I can hear are voices and sounds
Unfamiliar and scary to me.

The papers torn off and the lid is opened.
I can see lights and a little girl staring,
I look at her with my young puppy eyes,
She is not impressed!

Three days later here I am in the car on a quiet road,
It's dark here and silent.
The car has stopped.
I am thrown out.
I am sitting here bewildered and terrified.
What am I to do?

I can see a warm house with people in.
They are round a glowing tree.
I wish I was with them.
I hear footsteps; I cower into a bush.

There's a big dog and a farmer.
He picks me up with his wrinkly warm hands
And carries me into his house.
The warmth comforts me
And I know this is my new home.

Remember: a dog is for life not just for Christmas!

Chantal Greenfield (11)
Millais School

Go Away

What was that?
Who's there?
Go away! Leave me alone!
I hear footsteps . . .
Lots of footsteps . . .
Help! Please! Help!
Dust is seeping under the doors
All my priceless possessions are smashing to pieces!
Voices! I hear . . . voices!
They're lifting up my tomb lid!
Go away!
They dropped me!
Only the curse can stop them now!
I'm helpless and scared!
I just wanted them to go away . . .

Anna Betts (11)
Millais School

All Alone

I am all alone on an empty shelf,
A price tag through my ear,
People come so very near,
And leave me here with a golden tear.

When the sun comes out to shine
My fur is shown to be gold and fine,
Warm hands clutch my empty stomach,
Say bye-bye to this everyday havoc.

Tucked inside a warm cosy bed
To talk to I have my friend called Ted
He is just so very kind
And listens to what's going through my mind.

As the years go fast away
I am all alone in a pile of hay,
Who wants to listen to a bear
Who had a good time
But without a voice
Is gone and out of mind.
Because I am just a simple cuddly bear
Who has lost a lot of his golden hair.

Francesca Martin (11)
Millais School

The Old Ted's Fantasy

I have travelled through ages,
Through seas and skies,
Seen many planets at all different times,
I'm fluffy and cuddly,
You take me to bed,
What am I? I'm a teddy of course.

I am ripped and I'm torn, my ear is bitten,
I was born in the year 100bc,
I'm tiny and gold, I'm little and old,
I live in a massive house,
I sit on a bed all day long until it is 7pm,
Until my owner comes up to bed.

I love singing and dancing,
I love giggling and prancing,
But the best of all is at night,
All day I wait eagerly until it is time to lay down,
I get cuddled and loved by my owner,
Then *bang!* this is the worst part, I fall to the ground.

I wake up and remember all that I have done,
I think about ancient Egypt and the Greeks,
My owner back there was Miss Rebecca Ledger,
What about the Victorians, well Ruby was bad,
You should have seen what she talked about,
And the hole through my neck was from WWI.

Now I'm coming to an end of my beautiful life,
I will only live a few more days until I get burnt,
I loved every minute of it,
Especially when I fought in World War I,
The Battle of Hastings was great,
Ching, ching, bang, bang, and now I will go.

Lucy Brogan (11)
Millais School

Illusion

Darkness, the ultraviolet lights give the room an eerie effect
as I hold on tightly to my gun.
The bells chime as I run into the battle station.
Darting in and out of the dark figures I find a wall to hide behind.
I aim my heavy gun at the flickering lights and fire!
Thick smoke drifts through the laser beams.
Gunshots echo through my body
and beads of sweat drip from my palms.
Still grasping onto my gun I make a run for it.
Suddenly my belt moans in a rundown way
and my lights flash uncontrollably.
I have been shot.
The sirens go off again and I head for the exit.
I push myself through the stiff door and into the hall.
I pick up my party bag and head home.

Leanne Gaffney-Berkeley (11)
Millais School

On The Streets

T he whole world is against me,
H omeless, crying and upset,
E mpty feeling inside of me.

W orried about the rest of my family,
O n my own, always alone,
R unning in my bare feet to get scraps of food,
L eft on my own, hated,
'D umb', 'useless' are the cruel words I hear

I cry for all I'm worth,
S eeing I'm only 10.

A ll against me, hating me,
G loomy shapes hiding in the shadows.
A lleyways cold and dark,
I n hiding I stay, abandoned and scared,
N o one caring for me.
S lowly dying,
T ime taking as long as it can.

M e hungry, cold, poor and tired,
E ternal hunger is all I'm given in return.

Nicola Beverton
Millais School

Refugee

R efugee in Afghanistan
E veryone ignores her
F ar away from home
U nderstands what others like her feel
G unshots echo around her
E veryone has faces full of sorrow
E xcitement has faded, for now there is a war

I nside she feels cold and unwanted
N ever smiling, never joyful

A mericans pass, they look at her in sympathy
F ear is all she can think of
G asping every now and then
H oping for peace, she watches the soldiers
A gain another bomb explodes
N othing can stop her life being turned upside down
I nnocent people peer out from their shelters
S cary soldiers pass
T he bombing doesn't stop
A nother day will pass
N o one can stop people crying out with pain.

Sarah Benstead (11)
Millais School

Animals

A nimals are everywhere, sharing our world,
N orth, south, east and west, in the hot or cold,
I n the forests of the Amazon, or the seas of the pole,
M aking homes in rivers, trees, nests and even holes,
A lthough we're meant to share
L ife is rather bare
S o up and down and all around we have to show we care.

Katie Johnston (11)
Millais School

The Refugees' Plea

Echoing voices,
Freaky screams,
I am nothing to this strange country it seems,
I call for help but no one's there,
Where is this happy life we're supposed to share?

Where's the love within this world?
Freedom is all we want,
But nobody will listen.

Take the time to listen to our views,
Put yourself in our shoes,
All we want is to be respected,
Your love is not being reflected,
Take the time to talk to us,
For we must be set free.

Heather Craig (11)
Millais School

Homeless

I'm cold and lonely sitting on the street,
I have no place to go.
I'm sad and hungry sitting on the street,
I've never felt this low.
I'm tired and lonely sitting on the street,
How did I end up here?
I'm wet and dirty sitting on the street,
All I feel is fear.
I'm damp and smelly sitting on the street,
Why did this happen to me?
I'm ashamed and embarrassed sitting on the street,
Why can't anybody see?
I'm cold and lonely sitting on the street,
I have no place to go.
I'm sad and hungry sitting on the street,
I've never felt this low.

Amy Attwater (12)
Millais School

City Cat Culture

The cats who are feared by every soul,
They're the leaders of the city,
Emma, Fighter, Claws and Lol,
The ninjas who see everywhere.

Our group, we've had enough,
Me, Oscar, Tamara and Berty Bunny,
We're not at all mean but we are extremely strong,
Berty, the warden and us, the fighters.

We've had enough of the voodoo cats,
But they're the top fighters and extremely tough,
But we must fight them and that is that,
In order to stop them wiping out house cats.

We prepared that evening for a huge scram,
Berty was gathering bandages,
Getting ready were me, Oscar and Tam,
For the biggest fight of our lives.

We approached their turf confidently,
And waited for them to appear,
They came out confidently,
The fight began, although we cowered back in fear,
Oscar was the first cat down,
And soon after was Tamara,
I'd be beaten out of town!
But then my rabbit friend emerged.

Berty, our warden had healed many a cat,
But he'd beaten the life out of others,
Together, we defeated all but Emma,
But without her guards, she fled.

And now we'd done it with teamwork, hooray!
And all four of us are heroes to this day.

Sophy Morrow (11)
Millais School

The Victim

She pushes and punches,
She kicks and she slaps.
I run and hide away,
I can't fight back.

I tell nobody,
Of what she does to me.
I live in fear, hoping,
That one day she'll cease.

I'm covered in bruises,
All blue, black and red.
I look up to her eyes,
And wish I was dead.

Ashley Kidgell (12)
Millais School

Cast Aside

My mummy cat had kittens,
Not one, not two, but four.
When they are unhappy she licks them,
Hugs, cuddles and more.

My mummy never licked me,
And I never went miaow!
But I would do anything for her to hug me,
This week, right here, right now.

But it's never going to happen,
She lives too far away.
So instead I whisper to my cat,
And my sorrows go away.

Why are most children so lucky?
No worry, no fear, no fright.
But unfortunately I have all of these,
With me day and night.

Sometimes I feel jealousy,
Bursting through my chest.
Knowing to my mummy,
I'm not even second best.

When my mummy left us,
I was a toddler, maybe before,
But one thing is for sure,
I will love her for evermore.

Joanna Canham (12)
Millais School

The Stray

Chucked out, alone,
Nobody who cares,
Dreaming of a juicy bone,
But that wish just rips and tears.

I once had an owner,
I once had a friend.
Her name, Little Miss Jonah
I thought it would never end.

Two kind fair-haired girls
Found me and took me home
Their house full of china and shiny pearls,
They gave me a bath,
They gave me a comb.

It is hard to think that I was ever alone.

Amelia Ross (11)
Millais School

Nothing

What is nothing?
It's what's left in my purse after a trip downtown.
It's what's in my head when I go into school . . .
And what remains after.
It's what I think of boys . . .
And football and chores . . .
It's how much I read on some days,
And how much I sleep on some nights.
It's my dad's usual score in cricket
And how many I score in netball.
It's what you find in the middle of a Polo,
And what's left after a scrummy, yummy Indian meal.
So - what can nothing be?
Anything and everything!

Jessica Speller (11)
Millais School

The Blind Man

Endless darkness there is for me,
Only because I cannot see.
I sit in my house all day long,
While I listen to the birds sing their song.
I'd love to walk through my door,
Just to see the world once more.
Being blind is a misery,
Oh, if only I could see.
There's so many things in the world to view,
This is a sad poem for me and you.

Jasmine Boyce (11)
Millais School

I, The Blinded Child

Hear? I can.
Feel? I can.
Smell? I can.
Taste? I can.
See? I cannot.

Blinded,
To the reflection in the mirror.
Blinded,
To the trees in the meadow.
Senseless to the visual beauties in life.
What's God done to me?
Why did I deserve such treatment?
Such a disability placed upon my life.
Why? Why? Why me?

Hear? I can.
Feel? I can.
Smell? I can.
Taste? I can.
See? I cannot.
Born senseless.
Why? Why? Why me?

Roya Mandegaran (11)
Millais School

Evacuee

Travelling

On the train crying,
I sit, scared
The maid comes round, smiling

Quivering

Will someone like me?
Love me fair?
Am I here forever?

Imagining

My new family,
Kind or strict?
I wish I could be home

Shivering

The cold air brushes
Against me,
Snow falling on the ground

Rejoicing

Running to Mother,
And Father.
War is gone at last!

Briony Munslow (12)
Millais School

Abandoned

No! Come back,
Can anyone hear me?
No! Don't go,
I don't understand.

Please don't leave me,
What have I done?
It was all a mistake,
Don't go.

No one to love me,
No one to care.
Why have you abandoned me,
Left me sitting here?

But no one can hear me,
No one will explain.
I'm all on my own now
Wondering
Watching
Waiting.

Kate Wilkinson (11)
Millais School

The World Cup Final

It's the World Cup final,
I can't believe I'm here,
We're in the changing room,
All I can hear is cheering.

We're lining up to go on the pitch,
The ref's reminding us of the rules,
I'm really, really nervous,
I've never felt it before.

I lead my team out in determination and pride,
Drums are banging and horns are tooting,
The atmosphere is amazing,
I'm really, really excited.

We line up for out national anthem,
Everybody's singing,
I'm proud to be representing my country,
I hope I don't let them down . . .

Molly Eade (12)
Millais School

A Life Of Darkness

I look, straining my eyes to catch a glimpse
of some wonderful rainbow world
but all I see is darkness.

I search, trying desperately to find someone
or something that can help me out of this prison
but all I see is darkness.

I reach out, hoping to find a miracle
that will chase away my loneliness
but all I see is darkness.

I am trapped inside my own head,
and people don't know what it's like for me
in a bleak world of velvety blackness.

I can hear sounds around me,
but they are meaningless and overwhelming.

What is colour?
What is light?
What is beauty?

I feel so alone.

Matilda Wraith (11)
Millais School

My Doggy Days

I'm small, I'm cute, I'm not quite 3,
Next-door's cat is not safe with me.
She sits on the wall,
My barking starts.
As soon as she sees me,
She shoots off like a dart.
Life is fun.

I spy my blue lead and hear my call,
My heart does a flip and I sprint for the hall.
The smells of the street are exciting and new,
My coat is wet with morning dew.
Life is fun.

On my back with my legs in the air,
I snore and dream without a care,
Until the bell rings at half-past three,
When I know someone's home to play with me.
Life is fun.

Emily Gardiner (11)
Millais School

The Red Dragon

I'm going on a scary ride
I feel nervous and excited
As we go through the tunnel
To get to the Red Dragon.

I sit down on the seat
My stomach in my feet
Now I'm locked in
I cannot change my mind.

We are moving
Whoosh wee!
Yippee argh!
The nervousness was gone
All I feel is happiness again.

Gabrielle Oake (11)
Millais School

Singing Competition

Sitting down quietly, rehearsing my lines,
doing this for my family for all good times.

I walk into the room, hiding my face,
as I stagger into my place,

I open my mouth, nothing comes out,
I have no idea what it's all about.

I try again in desperation,
then run to the door in devastation.

Anna Ward (11)
Millais School

The Seasons

In spring I feel happy
New life all around
The small birds singing
In the tall green trees

In summer I feel hot
And swim all day
With the sun shining
Down on me I happily play

When autumn comes I see leaves
Turn and feel the air grow cooler
With Bonfire Night on its way
Fireworks light up the sky

Now winter's here I step outside
And play in the cold winter snow
With freezing hands and frostbite toes
I come inside to warm my nose.

Nicola Skelton (11)
Millais School

Why?

What am I doing?
Where am I?
The man in the coffin and the terrible lie.

The thoughts I am thinking,
The words I may pray,
Cannot undo what happened yesterday.

Was it my fault?
What did I do?
I only remember my life with you.

For I am only a child,
I wouldn't ask much,
To be painfully blessed with our very last touch.

But now I feel scared,
All on my own,
Because now you have left me,
I feel so alone.

Hannah Jones (11)
Millais School

Pencil Case

Sitting on a desk I'm all alone,
Waiting,
Waiting.

All my life I've spent sitting here,
No one to talk to,
No one to listen to.

Always opening,
Then closing once more,
Nothing to do but wait.

After the lesson I sit in a bag,
Suffocated by books,
Once again a bumpy ride.

Then we get home,
Still nothing to do,
Alone.

Hollie Thomas (12)
Millais School

Hedgehog Worries

Winter's come,
The sky's glistening white, snow is falling fast
Sitting here shivering cold and wet
The morning's arrived
I must get moving
But what to do first?
I'll collect my food
I look and look but nothing
Not a slug or woodlice in sight
Now to dig my hole
Out of sight of predators
At last my hole is dug, but still no food
I look again but still nothing
I give up and pick some berries
Then taking one last look outside
I slip into my new home
Time to sleep
Goodnight.

Emma Griffith (12)
Millais School

Being Famous

I am a famous actress,
Right now I'm starring in a Hollywood film,
I have been in loads of popular programmes
And met thousands of famous actors.

I love my job, as I get paid millions!
It's great giving everyone my autograph,
I get around everywhere in a limo
And I always find myself on the red carpet!

I feel happy that I got a good job,
And can afford everything expensive I need,
I'm so glad I enjoy my life,
I love being an actress! I love being famous!
I love being me!

Eleanor Simpson (11)
Millais School

Earth's Wrath

They think they are so clever,
But who cares if they put Man on *my* moon?
Who cares if they put Man on the top of *my* highest mountain?
Computers and rockets can't stop me,
One flick of my green wrist and they will be gone,
All gone.

They chop down my amazing forests,
Poison my flowing rivers,
And kill my beautiful creations,
I am the only,
The only person which has stopped this dismal planet
From being destroyed,
But I can easily stop.

One stamp of my feet and a rumbling earthquake
Will plunge this planet into turmoil,
One touch of a finger and a volcano will erupt,
Covering this world with lava and ash,
One clap of my hands and a roaring tsunami
Will soak the earth to the core.

These people have disturbed my world for too long,
They have one last chance,
One last chance to clean up their act,
After all, no one messes with Mother Nature.

Joanna Nayler (12)
Millais School

Butterfly Poem

Most people look at me as if I'm the butterfly queen
which I would love to be.

I fly above everyone and everything
sweeping like a free spirit in the fresh, sweet air.

Every person compliments me on my colourful wings
as I fly gently and carefully by my own rules.

My little mind tells me what to do but no one is in charge of me
apart from my pretty wings, swifting me this way and that.

Zoë Meeks (11)
Millais School

School Uniform

I hang inside a young girl's closet,
Waiting there for my turn.
At 7 o'clock I'm up and ready,
To go dashing around there and learn.

At 9 o'clock it's time to go,
I'm energetic and ready for the day.
I arrive at last, bang on time,
What's my next lesson and which way?

My favourite subject of these 6 hours,
Yes, it's time for art, hip hip hooray.
Luminous colours and messy paint,
I'd have this subject any day.

I finally make my way through the hustle and bustle,
To get in line for my bus,
Realising what a great day I've had,
I must come back I must, I must!

I'm tired and drowsy after that day,
So now I go back in my closet and hide away.

Eve Danbury (11)
Millais School

Lost And Found

Here I stand all on my own,
With nothing more than a lead and a bone.

I have been standing here for what seems like years,
Holding back lonely tears.

Passers-by come and go,
But no one ever says hello!

Until one day I heard a noise
It sounded like a gang of boys.

One stopped, knelt down and looked at me,
And I stared up at him with glee.

Was this the one to take me home,
Or would he leave me here alone?

He called someone on his phone,
And spoke to a lady whose name was Joan.

She came to me and gave me a hug,
Then took me home and made me warm and snug.

Emily Lord (11)
Millais School

A Nurse's Thoughts And Feelings

A nurse must have many thoughts
whilst she is working.
Such as hoping her patients get well soon,
praying that no emergencies come in,
feeling proud of the work she is doing,
healing the sick.

Sometimes feeling happy and sometimes sad,
thinking of when she finishes her shift to go home
and put her feet up and rest before her next shift starts.

Kathryn Taylor (11)
Millais School

Tiger

Stealthily stalking his prey.
Never wavering.
Never losing sight of his target.

Tiger is weak, so weak,
Can he carry on?
He has lost everything to poachers.
His family, his land.

Rustle, rustle,
What's that?
Tiger looks round.
Nothing there.
He carries on.

Bang!
Tiger's hurt.
Someone comes out of the bushes.
Poachers.
He roars.

Then nothing.
Just black.

Rebecca Hollands (12)
Millais School

A Day In The Life Of A Penny

I've been dropped down the drain,
I've been out in the rain,
I've been picked up again,
I've been left on a train.

I've been dropped in the street,
I've been trodden on with feet,
I've been given as a treat,
I've been left on a seat.

I've been left in a car,
I've been stuck in a jar,
And you didn't think
I went very far.

Lizzie Harman (11)
Millais School

My Dragons

My dragons' names are Ged and Fred,
They are twins and they are both green with red eyes.
One can turn red with green eyes,
But I can't tell which one.
I wish I could because they tell me to do lots of things.
One tells me to go out and play or do my homework (all good things)
But the other one tells me to do no homework,
Be nasty and mean and very bad stuff.
I don't listen to that dragon.
Sometimes I get confused and argue with my dragon.
I wish that they were both the same and told me good things.

Sarah Porter (17)
Philpots Manor School

Rose The Dragon

Rose is as red as a rose.
Rose was born in a rose.
Rose lives as a rose most of the time.
Rose likes my cat, Bertie.
She likes pulling out his fur.
Rose is a dragon.

    Live as a rose,
    My dragon,
    Live as a rose.
    Please?

Rose likes to play pranks,
And get into trouble.
But when she's caught,
She just sits on my head,
Her tail round my neck.
Rose is my dragon.

    Live as a rose,
    My dragon,
    Live as a rose.
    Please?

Rose pulled Bertie's tail.
Bertie yells at her.
Rose pulled a scary face.
Bertie shot up the stairs,
And under his mum's bed.
Rose is a laughing dragon.

    Live as a rose,
    My dragon,
    Live as a rose.
    Please?

Emma Wint (17)
Philpots Manor School

Are We Fair?

Are we fair?
Do we dare?
To hurt animals
Over there
Do we dare?
Are we fair?
To hurt animals
Anywhere?
It's not fair
It's not fair
Do not dare
Do not dare.

Megan Simmonds (11)
Philpots Manor School

Young Writers Information

We hope you have enjoyed reading this book - and that you will continue to enjoy it in the coming years.

If you like reading and writing poetry drop us a line, or give us a call, and we'll send you a free information pack.

Alternatively if you would like to order further copies of this book or any of our other titles, then please give us a call or log onto our website at www.youngwriters.co.uk

**Young Writers Information
Remus House
Coltsfoot Drive
Peterborough
PE2 9JX**

(01733) 890066